THE CREED IN

THE CREED IN THE CATECHISM

The Life of God for Us

Eamon Duffy

continuum
LONDON • NEW YORK

Continuum

The Tower Building
11 York Road
London SE1 7NX, UK

15 East 26th Street
New York 10010
USA

www.continuumbooks.com

First published 1996
This edition published 2005

British Library Cataloguing-in-Publication Data
A catalogue record for this book is available from the British Library.

ISBN 0-8601-2398-7

'I Am the Great Sun' by Charles Causley, from *Collected Works* (Macmillan), reprinted by permission of David Higham Associates.

Extract from 'Was He Married?' by Stevie Smith, from *The Collected Poems of Stevie Smith* (Penguin 20th Century Classics), reprinted by permission of James MacGibbon.

'The Great Day', by W. B. Yeats, from *The Collected Poems of W. B. Yeats*, ed. A. Norman Jeffares (Macmillan), reprinted by permission.

Typeset by YHT Ltd
Printed and bound in Great Britain by
Biddles Ltd, King's Lynn

Contents

Introduction

This is not a book about the Creed, but about the way the Creed is presented to us in the *Catechism of the Catholic Church*. My aim in writing it is the modest one of helping those who use the Catechism to understand just what it is that the authors are saying, and to offer some critical grip on the way they say it. When in the sixteenth century a Catechism was commissioned to mediate the teaching of the Council of Trent, the last great pastoral council of the Church before our own age, the job was given to Dominicans. As a result, the Catechism of Trent had the coherence and consistency of a single theological school. Our Catechism, by contrast, is, like the camel, an animal designed by a committee. Within its pages will be found a range of emphases, theological perspectives and lines of approach, not always entirely consistent, and while trying to avoid jargon and a forest of footnotes, I have also tried to identify and assess these emphases where they seemed relevant to a clear understanding of the Catechism's message. Above all, I have tried to relate the contents of the Catechism to the teaching of the Second Vatican Council, which the Catechism exists to explain and mediate to a generation of Catholics for many of whom the Council itself is now at best a fast-fading memory. Pope Paul VI described the documents of Vatican II as 'the great Catechism of our age', and they of course remain normative for all interpretations of the Catechism. As I have tried to make clear, any conscientious catechist will often need to go behind the text of the Catechism to the conciliar documents on which it is based: it is to the words of the Council, and not the Catechism, that we must ultimately go to catch the definitive voice of the Holy Spirit for our age.

The Catechism was not intended, and is not entirely suitable, for direct use in the classroom, pulpit or study group. It was offered by the Pope to the bishops of the Universal Church as a resource, 'a point of reference for the catechisms or compendia that are composed in various countries'. But it was also intended to be read by priests, catechists and the faithful generally, and human nature being what it is, it is in fact now being used as a text-book in schools, RCIA groups and other catechetical situations. I have therefore written on this assumption, and have included material and comment intended to help in that context.

In a book this size it has not been possible to comment on every aspect of the Catechism's exposition of the Creed, but I have kept to its arrangement of material, which is that of the Creed itself, rather than rearranging it thematically. This makes for three dauntingly large chapters, but the retention of the Catechism's order and subheadings should make material on any given topic relatively easy to locate and use. One omission deserves comment. In general I have avoided comment on the 'in brief' sections which are provided as summaries of the discussion within each section. In the course of preparing the book I have come to the firm conclusion that these sections are likely to do more harm than good: they often oversimplify a nuanced and balanced discussion, and in some cases are downright misleading. They should be read attentively, handled with care, and never simply assumed to be an adequate summary of the preceding discussion.

Like any compendium, the Catechism has its weaknesses as well as its strengths, and I have tried to assist the reader to a sense of both. As I have worked on this book, however, my admiration for the achievement of the Catechism, and the riches of teaching and devotion which it makes available, has grown and deepened. The writing of this book has been for me a voyage of discovery and renewal in faith. It is my hope that it may help some at least of its readers in the same journey.

Cambridge,
Feast of the Assumption 1995

PART ONE

I Believe in God the Father

I BELIEVE — WE BELIEVE (26–175)

CHRISTIAN LIFE BEGINS with a question. At the outset of the baptismal rite the priest demands 'What do you ask of God's Church?' and the candidate replies 'Faith'. Faith is the cornerstone of the Christian life, and so the Catechism opens with an extended discussion of faith and its content, based round the Apostles' Creed, the ancient baptismal creed of the Roman Church. Yet this way of starting was by no means a foregone conclusion. In the immediate wake of the Second Vatican Council the Dutch bishops produced a new Catechism. Though it eventually ran into trouble with the authorities in Rome, this 'Dutch Catechism' was in many ways the forerunner of the new Catechism of the Catholic Church, for it was the first systematic attempt by any conference of bishops to apply the insights of the Council to the whole of Christian life and belief, the first Catechism of the Council.

Unlike the new Catechism, however, this controversial Dutch Catechism did not begin with the Creed or with the nature and content of faith. Instead, its first chapter was a discussion of the human religious quest, entitled 'The mystery of existence', with sub-headings like 'Man the questioner', 'The immense longing', 'The call for the infinite'. Chapter 2 continued this human-centred emphasis with a discussion of world religions (including Marxism) and it was only with chapter 3 that the Catechism got down to discussion of revelation, in a chapter on the religion of ancient Israel.[1]

It is not difficult to see why the authors of the Dutch Catechism chose to begin their book in this way. Catechisms are for religious learners and religious seekers, and so there is an obvious case for beginning with the religious stirrings and questions which have brought such seekers to the Catholic Church. There has already been a good deal of criticism of the new Catechism precisely for its failure to make this sort of concession, criticism which, as we shall see, has some foundation.

And yet to begin an exposition of the Catholic faith with a discussion of the human religious quest, as the Dutch Catechism did, was in a sense to put things round the wrong way, and in the process unwittingly to betray one of the fundamental theological emphases of the Council itself. For the Council, like the New Testament, insisted that human encounter with God is *always* the work of grace, always the result of God's own self-giving. Faith is not a reaching out into the dark, but a response to a divine summons which calls humanity into the light of knowledge of and friendship with the God who creates, redeems and sanctifies. The invisible God, 'from the fullness of his love, addresses men as his friends . . . in order to invite and receive them into his own company'.[2] To *start* with humanity's religious quest can make sense as a practical strategy, but it may also help to obscure the deeper reality that in the end we seek God only because, from the beginning, he seeks us with a Father's love.

That is why the new Catechism insists from the start that belief in God arises not from our search for God, but from God's loving search for us. Faith, the human response to the God who reveals and gives himself to us, is itself the free gift of God, and our hunger for God is an appetite placed in our hearts as a clue to lead us home to him (26, 153). That idea goes back at least to St Augustine, in a famous appeal to God which is quoted by the Catechism – 'You have made us for yourself, and our heart is restless until it rests in You' (30). The seventeenth-century Anglican priest-poet George Herbert turned that sentence into an unforgettable poem. What we experience as a deep-seated fact of human nature, our longing for God, is in fact, Herbert explains, God himself drawing us to him – his longing for us: so Herbert's poem is called 'The Pulley'.

> When God at first made man,
> Having a glass of blessings standing by;
> Let us (said he) pour on him all we can:
> Let the world's riches, which dispersed lie,
> Contract into a span.
>
> So strength first made a way;
> Then beauty flowed, then wisdom, honour, pleasure:
> When almost all was out, God made a stay,
> Perceiving that alone of all his treasure
> Rest in the bottom lay.
>
> For if I should (said he)
> Bestow this jewel also on my creature,
> He would adore my gifts instead of me,
> And rest in Nature, not the God of Nature.
> So both should losers be.
>
> Yet let him keep the rest,
> But keep them with repining restlessness:
> Let him be rich and weary, that at least,
> If goodness lead him not, yet weariness
> May toss him to my breast.

So, although the first chapter of the Catechism is indeed headed 'Man's capacity for God' and deals with the human religious quest, it opens with a resounding quotation from the Council which sets out the claim that our search for God is God's own gift to us:

> The dignity of man rests above all on the fact that he is called to communion with God. This invitation to converse with God is addressed to man as soon as he comes into being. For if man exists it is because God has created him through love, and through love continues to hold him in existence. He cannot live fully according to truth unless he freely acknowledges that love and entrusts himself to his Creator.[3]

Following the teaching of the First Vatican Council the Catechism does indeed insist that we can know of God's existence by the use of our reason alone, for how else could we begin to speak of him? But its real centre of interest is in the response of human beings in faith to God's definitive self-revelation in Jesus Christ. Most of the thirty pages of this first Section of the Catechism are devoted to a discussion of what it means to have faith in this more explicit sense, and to a discussion of the nature of revelation as we encounter it in the Scriptures and the preaching of the Church. Though human reason can enable us to acknowledge the reality of God's existence, the Catechism emphasizes the limitations of such knowledge, and the 'many obstacles' which prevent 'the effective and fruitful use of this inborn faculty'. Instead it emphasizes the obedience of religious faith, which demands not cool rational calculation but 'self-surrender and abnega-tion' (37).

Catholics used to talk less often of faith than of 'the Faith', meaning by that the collection of beliefs that make up Catholicism. The Catechism's teaching is altogether richer and more biblical. Faith is no mere intellectual assent to a set of beliefs. It is first and foremost the 'personal adherence' of the whole person to God, a free and loving response which is wholly ours, involving our reason, understanding and will, and which is yet an undeserved gift, springing not from 'flesh and blood', but from the Father himself, moving and convert-ing our hearts by his Holy Spirit. The models of our faith are Abraham, whom the canon of the Mass calls 'our father in faith', and Mary. Abraham's faith was a venture into the unknown, the loving trust in God that carried him and his out of the familiar homeland, to wander as strangers and pil-grims. Mary's unwavering response to the promise of God in the Incarnation perfectly embodies the obedience of faith (144–149). Both of them point us towards Jesus Christ, whom the epistle to the Hebrews calls 'the pioneer and perfecter of our faith' (165). And though faith is a personal and free act, it is not an isolated act. 'No one can believe alone, just as no one can live alone.' To believe in God is to receive the good news from others, and to share it in our turn. Individual

Christians take their place in 'a great chain of believers', a cloud of witnesses (166).

So, to have faith is much more than to hold a set of opinions, however strongly. It is to give one's whole life in love and trust. We talk of keeping faith, of being faithful in marriage, and it is that deeper meaning of belief which the Catechism commends to us. St Augustine sums up this rich and many-layered understanding of faith when he writes 'What is it to believe in [Christ]? It is believing to love him, it is believing to delight in him, it is believing to journey towards him, and to be gathered into his body.'[4]

Faith, then, is 'another order of knowledge' from mere rational belief that the world owes its origin to a creator. The gift of faith is the response to revelation, which, traced from the earliest origins of Israel in the patriarchs, is itself a manifestation of God's tireless love for humankind. God's self-revelation culminates in the final and complete self-giving of God in Christ, God's final Word, and his only Word. Truly to hear that Word is to recognize that God has nothing to say to us that is not love. As St Paul says,

> For the Son of God, Jesus Christ . . . is not Yes and No; but in him it is always Yes. For all the promises of God find their Yes in him. That is why we utter the Amen through him, to the glory of God.[5]

Our Amen, the 'Yes' of faith, is itself evoked by the prior and eternal 'Yes' of God in Christ, who calls us into being, and into friendship, out of love. That Word is transmitted to all times and all people in the Scriptures, and in the doctrine, life and worship of the Church, referred to here under the blanket term 'Tradition'.

The teaching of the Catechism here is closely modelled on one of the Council's most important documents, the Dogmatic Constitution on Revelation, *Dei Verbum*. In particular, it faithfully reproduces *Dei Verbum*'s insistence on the unity and harmony of Scripture and Tradition. One of the disastrous consequences of the religious divisions of the sixteenth century was the development of a false conflict between Bible and Church. Reformation theologians, afraid that God's Word had been smothered by human corruptions and superstitions, isolated the Scriptures as the sole source of knowledge of the Gospel, and set it above and over against the official Church. Catholic theologians, in reaction, exalted the Church's authority, minimized the role of the Bible in the life of the individual Christian, and discouraged lay access to the Scriptures. Both ways of proceeding proved disastrously one-sided, and the Catechism, following the Council, rejects this false polarity, insisting that Tradition and Scripture are both vital and complementary expressions of the one mystery of Christ. The apostolic tradition has come down to us in a special way in the written Scriptures, but it is also present and complete in the living tradition of the Church, embodied in her worship, articulated in her doctrines, expressed in the lives and prayers of the faithful. Scripture and Tradition are not rivals, but go together as twin expressions of the one and undivided Word of God, revealed in the person of Jesus Christ.

The Catechism has a great deal to say about Scripture, which, following the Council, it sees as fundamental to every aspect of the life of the Church. Scripture, it insists, is to be venerated on a par with the Blessed Sacrament (103), for it is 'the power of God for salvation to everyone who has faith', the foundation of all Christian teaching, especially in the liturgy, the 'very soul of sacred theology', and the basis of the individual Christian life. In contrast to the Counter-Reformation Church's nervousness about lay Bible-reading, the Catechism insists that the Scriptures 'ought to be open wide to the Christian faithful' – 'Ignorance of the Scriptures is ignorance of Christ' (131, 133).

All this part of the Catechism's teaching is closely paraphrased from the wonderfully rich sixth chapter of *Dei Verbum*, but it does not always manage to convey the full message of the original, and more than most parts of the Catechism, this section needs to be read alongside its original source. The Catechism's summary omits *Dei Verbum*'s strong encouragement of Catholic biblical scholarship, and of ecumenical translation and study of the Bible, not least *Dei Verbum*'s insistent emphasis on the need for all those engaged in Christian ministry to undertake serious and continuous biblical study. The authors of the Catechism are clearly a good deal more nervous than the Council Fathers about asserting the authority of the Scriptures over the Church as 'the fundamental rule of her faith', and the Catechism's discussion of methods of interpreting the Scriptures in accordance with the mind of the Church seems timid and even in places somewhat eccentric. *Dei Verbum* encouraged Catholic biblical scholarship, using all 'appropriate methods'. This encouragement was taken up in 1993 by the Pontifical Biblical Commission in a document entitled *The Interpretation of the Bible in the Church*, written thirty years on from the Council, and designed to draw out the implications of *Dei Verbum* in the light of a whole generation of remarkable development in Catholic biblical studies. This document makes it clear that the 'appropriate methods' encouraged in the Council's text can and should include all the resources of modern biblical study. Catholic biblical exegetes have the same responsibilities and the same rights to intellectual honesty and scientific rigour in their work as their non-Catholic colleagues, with whom they are encouraged to co-operate. Catholic exegesis differs only in taking place within the 'living tradition of the Church', and with the consciousness of the 'ecclesial task' of helping pastors and people to explore the riches of Scripture. *The Interpretation of the Bible in the Church* has been widely welcomed, inside and outside the Church, as a remarkably comprehensive, open and positive statement of the responsibilities and legitimate freedoms of the biblical scholar within the Church.[6] It is a million miles away from the early-twentieth-century utterances of the Pontifical Biblical Commission, which were all too often a disastrous series of Canute-like attempts by the authorities to stamp out any study of the Bible which might threaten received opinion. The Catechism, unfortunately, seems inclined to return to the nervous attitudes of the pre-conciliar period, and to walk on eggshells here. It does indeed recognize that the books of the

Bible are ancient texts with human authors, and that in reading them we need to take account of the 'conditions of their times and culture'. But the Catechism offers as the essential key to interpreting the Bible not the methods and resources of modern scholarship, but the medieval fourfold senses of Scripture, the literal sense, the allegorical sense, the moral sense, and the anagogical sense. A rough translation of these would be 'What is the Scripture passage mainly about? Has it a lesson for us? How does it relate to Christ? How does it relate to the Christian hope?'[7] These questions clearly have a place in any Christian reading of Scripture, but they take no account of anything that has happened in the world of biblical studies for centuries, and there is a generally jumpy insistence throughout this section of the Catechism on the authority of the Church leaders over the work of biblical interpretation, which is markedly at odds with the more relaxed and less fearful tone of the Pontifical Biblical Commission's document, and indeed of *Dei Verbum* itself.

And that insistence on the role of the teaching authority of the Church, of the magisterium, colours and sometimes distorts a good deal else in this part of the Catechism. The account of faith in the Catechism acknowledges the centrality of free personal commitment and registers the inevitable presence of doubt and uncertainty in the life of believers (160, 163). But it emphasizes far more the objective content of faith, the things we must believe, and it lays more stress than the conciliar documents did on the role of the magisterium in directing the faith of believers. The Council's magnificent Constitution on the Church in the Modern World, *Gaudium et Spes*, had an extended and sympathetic discussion of atheism, despair and doubt in the human condition, seeing the riddle of human life as an enigma even for believers. From this perspective the Incarnation does not merely reveal God to man, it reveals to us what it is to be a human being, and the Council sees the Christian revelation as perfecting and completing truths which by the work of the Holy Spirit are present throughout human culture and human history. Christian faith has a great deal in common with what is best in human culture, and the Council insisted on the vital necessity of a fruitful dialogue between the Church and the world.

These emphases have largely been set aside in the Catechism. In stressing the centrality of the Jewish and Christian revelation, the Catechism both here and later, in what it has to say of the work of the Holy Spirit, pays little attention to the place of faith in a broader sense within human culture and religions. The Council had balanced its teaching in *Dei Verbum* on the centrality of God's self-revelation in Christ, with an insistence that the Spirit of God was at work in the whole of human history and human culture. The Council declared that all human beings are offered a share in the Paschal mystery, and called Christians to attend to the 'genuine signs of the presence or the purpose of God' outside the Church (*Gaudium et Spes* 11, 22).

This teaching is of course by no means straightforward or easy to understand. It raises enormous and complex questions about the status and value for salvation of other religions, and about the uniqueness of Christianity. Modern Catholic theologians have been deeply divided about what we are to say about righteous non-Christians, and how they are saved: Karl Rahner even wanted to talk of such people as 'anonymous Christians'.[8] Yet however it is understood, the Council's teaching offers the possibility of a more positive assessment of those religions. Sadly, the Catechism does not pursue this. It makes very little use of this crucial passage of *Gaudium et Spes*, and its discussion of faith is cast in explicit and even narrowly Christian terms, with a heavy emphasis on the teaching authority of Pope and bishops. In a book intended to shape catechesis for seekers from outside the Christian tradition as well as those already within it, this is a grave weakness, which users of the Catechism need to be alert to.

We can see the same insistence on hierarchy and authority in the account the Catechism gives of the handing on of apostolic tradition within the Church. The main source for the Catechism here is *Dei Verbum*, and it is worth giving the conciliar text at length.

> This sacred Tradition, then, and the sacred Scripture of both
> Testaments, are like a mirror, in which the Church, during its
> pilgrim journey here on earth, contemplates God, from whom
> she receives everything, until such time as she is brought to see
> him face to face as he really is.
> ... the apostles, in handing on what they themselves received,
> warn the faithful to maintain the traditions which they had
> learned either by word of mouth or by letter; and they warn
> them to fight hard for the faith that had been handed on to
> them once and for all. ... In this way the Church, in her
> doctrine, life and worship, perpetuates and transmits to every
> generation all that she herself is, all that she believes.

We need to note here the Council's emphasis on the role of the faithful in this process of transmission and protection of the truth – it is not the exclusive monopoly of the clergy or Church authorities. This emphasis is spelled out further as the paragraph continues:

> The Tradition that comes from the apostles makes progress in
> the Church, with the help of the Holy Spirit. There is growth
> in insight into the realities and words that are being passed on.
> This comes about in various ways. It comes through the
> contemplation and study of believers who ponder these things
> in their hearts. It comes from the intimate sense of spiritual
> realities which they experience, and it comes from the
> preaching of those who have received, along with their right of
> succession in the episcopate, the sure charism of truth. Thus,
> as the centuries go by, the Church is always advancing towards
> the plenitude of divine truth ...[9]

This is a marvellously balanced and subtle statement on the nature of tradition. It emphasizes the pilgrim character of the Church's journey through times and cultures, and its growth in insight and understanding. Above all it locates the process of tradition itself, the handing on, custodianship and deepening of Christian understanding, within the whole people of God. Tradition progresses through the study and the experience of *believers*, as well as from the preaching of the bishops.

They, the successors of the apostles, endowed with the 'charism of truth', do indeed have a distinctive role in the passing on and protection of the tradition, but *Dei Verbum* sets the role of the Church's pastors and teachers firmly in the context of the work of the whole body of the Church, which has a prophetic role in the discernment and preservation of Christian truth.

There is a marked contrast of tone and emphasis in the corresponding sections of the Catechism, where the emphasis is placed heavily on the responsibility and rights of the magisterium, meaning essentially the authority of the Pope, and where the role of the laity is seen as essentially passive – 'the faithful receive with docility the teachings and directives that their pastors give them in different forms' (87). The Catechism of course says nothing which cannot be found somewhere in the Council's documents, but in matters of delicate theological balance emphasis is everything, and its emphasis is significantly more hierarchical. Anyone using this section of the Catechism will need to read it alongside the far richer and more balanced conciliar texts on which it draws, and which, as the utterances of a General Council, of course carry infinitely greater weight than any Catechism.

THE PROFESSION OF THE CHRISTIAN FAITH

The creeds (185–197)

The Catechism casts its exploration of the Church's faith in the form of a commentary on the Apostles' Creed, supplemented with frequent reference to the Creed used at Sunday Mass, the so-called 'Nicene Creed'. But we should not imagine that this is because the Creed is primarily a handy list of the things Catholics must believe. Creeds are not *catalogues*, they are a prayerful proclamation of the bonds that join us in one. We mostly use the creeds in worship – above all at Mass. It is in prayer and praise that we call on God, Father, Son and Holy Spirit, when we begin with 'In the name of the Father', or end with 'Glory be to the Father. . .'.

The creeds are much fuller than either of these formulas, but like them they are intended not to itemize our opinions, but to celebrate the one God who has revealed himself as Father, Son and Spirit. Theologians used to debate how many 'articles' there were in the Creed. The commonest notion was that there were twelve, and an ancient legend told how the apostles gathered at Pentecost had contributed one article apiece. St Thomas Aquinas thought that there were fourteen, seven dealing with the Godhead and seven dealing with the humanity of Christ and its effects. The Catechism, however, tells us that there are just three articles in the Creed, devoted to Father, Son and Holy Spirit, like the doxologies with which we begin and end our prayer (190).

Both Greek and Latin have the same word for creed, *symbol.* Opinions differ about its origin, but it is probably connected with the tokens – usually a broken ring or seal or bracelet – which a messenger might present as a sign of identity. The broken piece would then be joined to its other half, establishing the identity and good faith of the newcomer, rather like spies in a modern thriller meeting and each producing one of the halves of a torn postcard. 'Symbol' was also the word used in the ancient mystery religions for the formulae by which members of the group recognized each other. St Augustine tells us that candidates for baptism at Rome had to stand in a high place and proclaim the Apostles' Creed – the Creed used here in the Catechism – before all the Church. The prologue to the Catechism tells us that 'those who belong to Christ through faith and Baptism must confess their baptismal faith before men' (14). This existential dimension of the Creed, not as a list of beliefs but as the sign and beginning of a new shared life in God, is what the Catechism seeks to emphasize. To explore the Creed is not to gather information, but to praise and bless the God who creates and cares for us, who heals and saves us, who draws us into love and unity with himself and with each other.

As on the day of our Baptism, when our whole life was entrusted to the 'standard of teaching', let us embrace the Creed as our life-giving faith. To say the Credo with faith is to enter into communion with God, Father, Son and Holy Spirit, and also with the whole Church which transmits the faith to us and in whose midst we believe. (197)

I believe in God (199–231)

The Catechism declares that belief in God, unique, one-only, is the most fundamental belief of all. The whole Creed speaks of this God, and all the other articles depend upon this one and are an expansion of it. To answer the question 'who is this one God?', the Catechism turns to God's self-revelation to Moses in the burning bush, and the communication of his Name, YHWH. The whole of the Catechism's treatment of this first article then takes the form of a meditation on the meaning of this Name.[10]

The Name is mysterious, 'as God is a mystery', at once 'a name revealed and something like a refusal of a name', thereby expressing what God is, infinitely above everything we can understand or say. He is *Deus absconditus*, a hidden God, and yet the one who makes himself close to human beings. The name therefore captures the paradox of God's majesty and his mercy.

It is also mysterious in part simply because we don't really know what it actually signifies. The Hebrew can be translated in a variety of ways – the Catechism explains it variously as 'I am who is', 'I am who am', 'I am who I am' . In fact many commentators think it means something more like 'He causes to be', a dynamic name which affirms God's creativity as his essence.[11] But for the authors of the Catechism the heart of this mysterious Name is its revelation that God alone IS, that he alone possesses the fullness of being and of every perfection, without origin and without end. All creatures borrow their existence from him, he alone is.

Revealing himself to Moses, God identifies himself as the God of all times. He is the God of the present – 'I AM'. He is also the God of the past, 'the God of your Fathers, the God of Abraham, the God of Isaac and the God of Jacob', and he is the God of the future – 'I will be with you'. Revealing his Name, he reveals his holiness – Moses takes off his shoes and veils his face before him, just as Isaiah cries out 'Woe is me, for I am a man of unclean lips',[12] and Peter cries out to Jesus, 'Depart from me, for I am a sinful man'. But he reveals himself also as infinitely compassionate. His holiness is not to cow and crush, but to redeem and raise up. And so St John can say that 'We shall reassure our hearts before him whenever our hearts condemn us, for God is greater than our hearts' (208). For the God of holiness and truth revealed to Moses is also the God revealed in Jesus Christ. Throughout St John's gospel Jesus is deliberately made to employ the Greek phrase *Egō eimi* – 'I AM', thereby claiming identity with the God of mercy and faithfulness who brought Israel out of Egypt.

To believe in this God, then, is not to assent to some philosophical abstraction, nor to bow down before some titanic energy whose majesty oppresses and terrorizes. It is to live in the joy and certainty of being loved, to know one's dignity as a child of God, and to know the unity of the human race in that dignity. It means recognizing that behind the good things of this world lies their creator, infinitely greater than them all and a more worthy of our love, and it means living in trust and hope, whatever adversity befalls us. The section concludes with a prayer of St Teresa of Avila, which expresses this loving trust in the one God :

> Let nothing trouble you
> Let nothing frighten you,
> Everything passes,
> God never changes
> Patience obtains all,
> Whoever has God
> Wants for nothing
> God alone is enough. (227)

The Father (232–267)

The Catechism insists that 'The faith of all Christians rests on the Trinity'. We are baptized in the name of Father, Son and Holy Ghost and, as we have seen, the invocation of that

Trinity is the beginning and the end of prayer. Christians do not believe in one God who is also, incidentally and bafflingly but rather abstractly, three. We know God *only* as he reveals himself to us as Father, Son and Spirit, and all our talk of God starts from our encounter with him in the life and person of his Son Jesus Christ, in whose Spirit we live. Yet although the doctrine of the Trinity stands as the centre and foundation of our faith, 'the mystery of God in himself' (234), it is often treated by Catholics as a burdensome conundrum which they would rather not hear about. Many clergy freely admit their dread of preaching on the subject, and parish congregations glaze over and think of Sunday lunch when the clergy do get round to it. It is a subject which has bred confusion and rank heresy among the ordinary faithful as well as among the theologians, a tendency not helped by the baffling opaqueness of much of the technical theological language of trinitarian formulae – 'substance', 'persons', 'hypostases'. The word 'persons', for example, applied to Father, Son and Holy Spirit, has left many Catholics with the utterly false idea that each of the persons of the Trinity is a different *personality*, with a distinct conscious mind and a separate centre of self-awareness, like three very close friends who agree about everything. This is a natural enough confusion, which some of the noblest expressions of the doctrine in art have helped to fix. The wonderful fifteenth-century icon of the Trinity by the Russian painter Andrei Rublev, for example, portrays the Trinity as the three heavenly beings ('angels') who visited Abraham at the oaks of Mamre (Genesis 18). Rublev's picture is one of the greatest of all Christian works of art, and his unforgettable image of the three angels gathered round the cup of Christ's supper and suffering explores the loving compassion within the mind and heart of God which brought about the Incarnation and Redemption. Yet, for obvious reasons, its symbolic representation of the Trinity as three people could also be misleading. In a different way, the once popular Western European representations of the Trinity as a man with three faces on one head set up different and equally misleading resonances, as if the Trinity was some monstrous sort of eternal schizophrenia in the mind of God.

Yet the element of puzzle or bafflement in trinitarian language about God can be overdone. The Trinity is a mystery because God is a mystery: all our language about him ends in the silence of adoration. Yet whether or not we are religious, the very structure of our own lives is trinitarian: whether we are aware of it or not, we are well used to talking about a single reality in three fundamentally distinct yet interlocking ways. In the first place, as human beings we are part of nature – in religious terms, of the creation – and the world around us, including our own bodies and brains, is part of the order of nature, the product of material forces. But secondly, we make sense of all that by using language, by describing it or telling stories about it; the stories of science or of history, for example, each in their ways offer accounts of reality which impose or uncover order within the brute reality of nature. And finally, we know ourselves and other people to be more than mere natural processes, or items within some story: we are personal beings, rejoicing, mourning, hating and loving, making music and making war, choosing and longing. So we experience the same single reality, the world of which we are parts, in three different ways: firstly as nature or creation, secondly as story, thirdly as personality. And if we experience the world in this trinitarian way, it is no surprise that our experience of God should arrange itself in this way too, as we recognize him as creator, as Word, and as lifegiver – Father, Son and Spirit – nor is it strange that the trinitarian character of the natural world should be a reflection of the trinitarian reality of its divine source.

There is a danger here, of course, that we will think of the Trinity *simply* as a convenient way of arranging our experience of God. One cause of impatience with the doctrine of the Trinity within Christian tradition has been a sense that it is a frivolous juggling with the unsayable, that it purports to tell us about the private life of God. Throughout Christian history there have been well-meaning attempts to spell out the meaning of the Trinity without claiming that in doing so we learn anything about the hidden reality of God. Such attempts speak simply in terms of God's action in the world, and see the distinction between Father, Son and Holy Spirit as applying only to God as he relates to us, as varying aspects of his work of creation and redemption, or even as mere ways of talking about our experience of the one God. The Fathers of the Church distinguished two dimensions of language about the Trinity, the language of the immanent Trinity, of *theology*, which describes God as he is in himself, and the language of the *'economic'* Trinity, which describes the works by which God reveals himself to us. Nevertheless, the Church, while recognizing that nothing we say about the mystery of God can measure up to the reality, has decisively rejected all attempts to reduce the doctrine of the Trinity to *mere* metaphor or symbol. 'Theology' and 'economy' must be held together, for they illuminate each other, and the Church believes that the language of Trinity does indeed tell us something about God as he really is, and not just as he appears to us. The Catechism helpfully points to an analogy with human behaviour – people disclose themselves by their actions, but equally, better knowledge of a person will enable us better to understand their behaviour (235–236).

We can get some sense why it is so important to insist that God really is Father, Son and Spirit, that he really *is* Trinity, if we reflect on the implications of some of the other language we use about him. At the heart of our belief in God is the conviction that not only is he supremely *loving*, but he actually *is* Love itself. The overwhelming love for us, disclosed in the Cross, tells us something absolutely fundamental about God, reveals his nature. Yet when did God begin to love? Does he love from all eternity, or only from the point at which he begins to create? Whom did God love before the world became? This is mythical language, but it poses a real question. Does God need his creation in order to be himself, is he incomplete without us? If so, then he does not create out of pure love and joy, he creates out of need. The Church has always rejected any such idea, and has affirmed that creation, like redemption, is pure grace. It is God's free gift out of his own overflowing richness and delight, not the scratching of some eternal itch, the fulfilment of his own needs (cf. 293). So, we are brought to recognize that in the heart of God there is *from all eternity* some unimaginably tender reality which corresponds to the complex of relationship, self-gift, understanding, and delighted sharing, which we call love: and to speak of this is to speak of Father, Son and Holy Spirit.

The doctrine of the Trinity was forced upon the Church as it struggled to do justice to what God had done for the world. It was forced to the recognition of the divinity of Christ, for it saw that only this enabled us to say that all that Jesus was and did reveals to us the mind and heart of God. It was forced, slowly and hesitatingly, to recognize the divinity of the Holy Spirit as it realized that only so could it proclaim its certainty that the new life of love and hope within the Church was God's own life recreating humanity. So the emergence of the doctrine of the Trinity was gradual, a painful and prolonged attempt truthfully to spell out the stupendous implications of the revelation of God in Jesus Christ. The Catechism sketches in some of the features of this process, though it tidies it up somewhat, and does not dwell on the element of trial and error which in fact characterized the turbulent and often confused early history of the Church (249–256). Nevertheless, it does emphasize the difficulty which the Church found in speaking of this great mystery, and the way in which the philosophical terms borrowed for the purpose had to be broken and reset: language had to be stretched and reinvented to hint at realities which were beyond human imagining (251). None of the claims we make about God is literally true, for he escapes all human language. We call him Father, yet he is mother to us too, and he is neither father nor mother. Words crumble and collapse in the face of the mystery of eternal love. We need to bear that salutary and humbling thought in mind whenever we are tempted to undue certainty or dogmatism in speaking of God.

The Creator (279–324)

Nowadays when creation is mentioned we tend immediately to think in scientific terms: the Big Bang, the expanding universe, the Primal Atom, all the issues which modern cosmology raises about the origins of our universe. And since at least the time of Galileo, it has been widely assumed, by scientists themselves as well as by bishops and theologians, that such questions invade the domain of the theologian, and might even challenge the Christian belief in creation. One of the best features of the Catechism's treatment of creation is that it will have none of this. It recognizes that scientific advance in this area may indeed have a religious dimension, but it identifies that religious dimension not as theological, but *doxological.* In plain terms, scientific advance in the field of cosmology may move us to greater wonder and praise at the might and wisdom of God. The scientist's understanding and knowledge is itself a product of the wisdom of God, which underlies all human enquiry (283). But the Church's faith in God as creator is of quite a different order: the question of creation is not a question about *how* things come to be the way they are, but a more fundamental question which science does not and cannot address. Why should there be any coherence or order at all, why should anything be in the first place? The doctrine of creation *ex nihilo*, out of nothing, does not mean that first of all there was nothing, and then God made something, it is not a matter of before and after. Creation *ex nihilo* means that creation is what we speak of when all explaining is finished. It is not the answer to the question 'How did things happen?' but 'What does it all *mean?*' The Bible and the Church have nothing whatever to tell us about how or when the universe started up. The creation stories in Genesis are not eye-witness accounts of the unimaginably remote past, in which the primal atom began to expand. They were written late in Israel's history and in mythological form by people who knew nothing about physics, to articulate Israel's belief that the world and all that therein is belongs to the God who heals and saves. In a crucial paragraph the Catechism tells us that the doctrine of creation is as much a question of our future as of our past, not merely 'What is our origin?' but 'What is our end?' (282).

St Thomas Aquinas thought that there was no philosophical reason why the world should ever have had a beginning, and the Christian doctrine of creation would not be affected if it could be shown that the universe had no discernible starting point. Instead, the doctrine of creation is an affirmation of God's immediate presence in and responsibility for the world. To believe in creation is to affirm that the world is indeed 'very good', that its existence and the order and harmony within it are God's gift, that suffering and sin are not part of his will for his creatures and will one day be overcome. The doctrine of creation is a recognition that the world exists for the glory of God and for our flourishing and 'beatitude' (294, 301). Nor does belief in creation deprive creatures of their freedom, or of their place as real agents in the world, for God's mode of presence and activity within creation is enabling and liberating for his creatures. He is not a force *within* the universe, competing with other forces, for he is creator, not a creature (306–308). Because of our belief in creation we can confront the evil in the world, recognizing its reality but confident that God is master of the world he makes, and that it is love which 'moves the Sun and the other stars'.[13]

The most striking aspect of the Catechism's handling of all this is its location of the doctrine of creation not in philosophical discussion, but within the context of salvation history, the *new* creation which is revealed in Christ. Creation is thus the foundation of 'all God's saving plans', the beginning of the history of salvation. Christ reveals the purpose of love and life which underlay God's creating work: 'from the beginning God envisaged the glory of the new creation in Christ'. Crucially, the Catechism locates its exposition of creation in the context of the Easter Vigil, with its majestic series of readings beginning with the first chapter of Genesis. The same covenant love which brought Israel out of slavery in Egypt, which rescued them from exile in Babylon, and which raised Jesus from the dead, underlies all God's dealing with his creatures (280, 288). Here the Catechism is very closely in tune with the biblical presentation of creation. The great celebration of God as creator in the Old Testament comes in the work of the prophet we call 'Deutero-Isaiah'. He wrote after the deportation of the Israelites to Babylon, and enabled them to hope again by recalling God's faithfulness to them in the desert, and from the beginning of the world. For the prophet, God's creating word is his saving word also, God is at once both creator and redeemer.

> Awake, awake, put on strength, O arm of the Lord;
> awake as in days of old, the generations of long ago.
> Was it not thou who didst cut Rahab in pieces, that didst
> pierce the dragon?
> Was it not thou that didst dry up the sea, the waters of the
> great deep;
> that didst make in the depths of the sea a way for the
> redeemed to pass over? . . .
>
> For I am the Lord your God
> who stirs up the sea so that its waves roar,
> the Lord of Hosts is his name.
> And I have put my words in your mouth,
> and hid you in the shadow of my hand,
> stretching out the heavens
> and laying the foundations of the earth,
> and saying to Zion, 'You are my people'.[14]

And it is in this context that the Catechism places our bewilderment and pain in the face of suffering and evil. Belief in creation is for Christians a part of their resurrection faith, born out of the experience of death and chaos. It is not some fatuous optimism, 'all for the best in the best of all possible worlds', for which the problem of evil is a fatal flaw, an embarrassment to be explained away. Belief in creation is affirmed not *despite* the existence of evil, but as the *answer* of faith to the enigma of evil. The *Fiat* of God in creation, the 'Yes' which calls the world into being, is the same 'Yes' spoken to us in the Cross and Resurrection, the 'Yes' that sounds on Easter morning from the empty tomb.

Only Christian faith as a whole constitutes the answer to this
question: the goodness of creation, the drama of sin and the
patient love of God who comes to meet man by his covenants,
the redemptive Incarnation of his Son, his gift of the Spirit, his
gathering of the Church, the power of the Sacraments . . .
there is not a single aspect of the Christian message that is not
in part an answer to the question of evil. (309)

After the third reading in the old pre-conciliar form of the
Easter Vigil there was an ancient prayer which summed up
this profound link between creation and redemption:

O God of unchangeable power and eternal light, look
mercifully on the wonderful mystery of your whole Church,
and by the tranquil operation of your perpetual providence
carry forward the work of human salvation. Let the whole
world see and feel that what was cast down is being raised up,
that what had grown old is being renewed, and that all things
are returning into unity through him from whom they took
their source, even Jesus Christ your Son, our Lord.

Heaven and earth (325–421)

To move from the Catechism's profound introductory treatment of the doctrine of creation to its handling of what it is
that God creates – heaven and earth, all that is seen and
unseen – is to experience something of a shock. These
paragraphs inevitably centre on the first three chapters of the
book of Genesis, fundamental texts for any exploration of
Christian reflection about the nature of humanity, and the
meaning and reality of sin. The authors of the Catechism
know and alert us to the fact that the Scriptures here are cast
in 'figurative language', yet, in marked contrast to the richness and depth of the Catechism's earlier treatment of God as
creator, much of the following discussion, and particularly
the treatment of the Fall, seems crude and almost fundamen-
talist in its handling of Scripture. Having earlier emphasized
the autonomy of science, the Catechism here tries to pre-
empt issues which can only be resolved, if at all, by the
methods of science, such as the question of whether the
whole of the human race is descended from a single pair of

ancestors. This section of the Catechism is likely to pose a lot of problems for those engaged in catechesis, particularly adult catechesis.

Heaven: the angels (328–336)

The tone of much else in this part of the Catechism is set by its discussion of the angels. God is creator of heaven as well as earth, and the Catechism tells us that this means that he is the Lord not merely of this world, but of our future destiny. God is the creator and Lord of the order of salvation, as well as of the order of nature. Also included in the notion of heaven, however, are the angels, and the Catechism devotes most of its space on 'heaven' here to an elaborate discussion of the angels. This is fair enough, for angels loom large in Scripture – as the members of the heavenly court of the Lord in Isaiah's temple vision 'in the year that King Uzziah died' (Isaiah 6), as the servants and messengers of God in countless biblical stories, not least those of the Annunciation and the Resurrection stories in the gospels, and as expressions of the all-caring providence of God, as in the book of Tobit or the stories of the temptations of Jesus. The angels, too, figure prominently in the liturgy, at the heart of the Mass itself, when in the Sanctus we join our earthly prayer and praise to the angelic liturgy before the face of God, and when in funerals we commit our loved ones into the care of the angels who will lead them into the company of the blessed. At the centre of this biblical and liturgical world of angels, the Catechism reminds us, is Christ: they are his angels, his messengers.

All this is an extremely rich and evocative language which speaks to us of God's transcendent power and glory, his loving care for us, his desire to speak to and save us. Christian prayer and reflection on the power and providence of God is saturated with language about angels, just as Christian art and literature have found some of their most memorable and profound imagery in angelology – Rublev's Trinity, Fra Angelico's Annunciation in San Marco's in Florence, Milton's archangels in *Paradise Lost*. It is hard to imagine Christian discourse emptied of all speech about angels. But we need to beware of literal-mindedness here. The language of Scripture, piety, art and liturgy does not always translate straightforwardly into the language of everyday fact: we are dealing here with a delicate web of metaphor and symbol, language for what we cannot otherwise say. The bald statement of the Catechism that 'The existence of the spiritual, non-corporeal beings that Sacred Scripture usually calls "angels" is a truth of faith' and that in this matter 'the witness of Scripture is as clear as the unanimity of Tradition' raises at least as many problems as it solves. The angels of the Old Testament, for example, like the flying creatures who cover their faces and their genitals with their wings in the vision of the heavenly court in Isaiah 6, hardly fit the later category of 'spiritual, non-corporeal beings'. They seem to be derived from non-Israelite Middle-Eastern mythologies, and they were part of the furniture of heaven in the conceptual world in which the Scriptures came to be written. They certainly tell us things we need to know about God – that he is awesomely great and holy, that he is to be worshipped, that he speaks to us, that he cares individually for each one of us every second of our existence – but exactly what we can deduce about their literal existence from the appearance of these courtiers or messengers of God in Scripture is another matter. There is no *literal* altar in heaven round which the angels gather, God does not *actually* sit on a throne supported by winged creatures: this is picture language, to express what cannot otherwise be said. The issue can be posed in the form of a question: do angels appear in Scripture to tell us something about angels, or to tell us something about God? If the latter, then we need to beware of quarrying the scriptural passages in which angels appear for nuggets of hard fact about the heavenly hierarchy.

And indeed we need only reflect for a moment to realize that in modern Catholicism the role of angels as messengers has virtually been abolished. Catholics still flock to holy places which have been, they believe, the scenes of divine messages. But in the overwhelming majority of cases the messenger concerned was not an angel, but a human being – the saints, above all the Blessed Virgin. There is a profound theological wisdom in all this, of which the Catechism reminds us by emphasizing that Christ is the centre of the angelic world. The great angel of God is not some created spirit, but his ultimate and perfect messenger, his Son. In our world the utterance and the providence of God is seen not in the angels and archangels, but in the face of Christ, and it is reflected from there in the faces of his human sisters and brothers. As Cardinal Newman declared in another context, 'Men, not angels, are the priests of God'.

Of course to deny the reality of the angels would be just as brash as it is to claim that the Bible gives us hard factual information about the existence and character of these marvellous beings. A reverend agnosticism seems appropriate here. But the Catechism's insistence that their existence is 'a truth of faith', a statement unqualified in any way, is likely to put unnecessary obstacles in the way of those who read what Scripture has to say of angels as the language of metaphor, of poetry. The Second Vatican Council recognized a 'hierarchy of truths' in the faith, and here if anywhere the authors of the Catechism should surely have registered that the 'truth of faith' under discussion might just possibly rank somewhat below that of the existence of God or the reality of the Resurrection. In catechesis we need to avoid making obstacles out of secondary issues.

The visible world (337–352)

By contrast with the problems raised in its treatment of the angels, the Catechism's short section on the visible world is strikingly rich and helpful. Much Christian discussion of the creation of the world has tended to use the language of domination, to see humankind as the sole purpose of creation, and to give to the non-human natural world no autonomous value. The Catechism wants to affirm the unique status of humanity as 'the summit of the Creator's work', but it lays great emphasis on the 'stability, truth and excellence' which every created thing has in its own right. Human beings must therefore respect both the autonomy and the interdependence of created things, must respect the diversity of creatures, and must not abuse the world in which we find ourselves, and of which we are a part. There is a solidarity of creatures which arises from their common origin in God, and their common ordering towards his glory. The Catechism invokes one of the first nature poems in European literature, St Francis of Assisi's 'Canticle of the Creatures', which celebrates God in all his creatures, whom it names the 'brothers and sisters' of the human race (344). This is all a refreshing change from traditional Christian emphasis on the 'dominion' which human beings had over other creatures, and clearly a new sensitivity to ecological and environmental concerns runs through this section, but it is not a mere grasping after fashion. The Catechism's teaching here is rooted in profound reflection on Scripture. The authors link all this to the purpose of creation which, they say, 'was fashioned with a view to the Sabbath' and therefore 'for the worship and adoration of God'. This insight, developed from the great hymn of creation in Genesis 1, which culminates in God's sabbath rest, rules out any merely human-centred view of the world. The creation exists not to feed humanity, but to worship God: all that is gives glory to God simply by being, and so its being is precious in God's purposes. The world is God's song of love, not humanity's factory or toy. More than that, the linking of creation to the sabbath raises profound questions about our understanding of our own place and function in the world, and of the meaning of work, for the sabbath rest in Genesis (and in the epistle to the Hebrews) is a glorious foretaste of the end towards which the whole world is moving, not the begrudged and minimalized interruption of trade and toil which it is in our culture. There is here a profound implicit criticism of our culture's values, and our assumptions about what it is that gives individuals in society their value.

Man – and Fall (355–421)

In its treatment of the 'Image of God' the Catechism seeks to emphasize both the unique dignity and the unique vocation of human beings. Both the dignity and the vocation are manifested in Christ, who reveals what it is to be truly human. Alone among living creatures, human beings are capable of knowing themselves and God, and so of entering into communion with him and with one another. Human beings are the priests of creation, offering it back to the Father in the name of all that lives – the Catechism is here paraphrasing a magnificent section of the conciliar text *Gaudium et Spes* (GS 14) and should be read alongside the richer original. This unique relationship with God is only fully revealed in Christ, and so it is in Christ that the 'mystery of Man becomes clear' (359). Humanity is made in Christ's image, so that the image of God might be perfected in us. The Catechism makes use of St Paul's language of the two Adams, one of the earth earthy, one spiritual. Humanity has thus two first Fathers, Adam and Christ, and Christ is in the deepest sense the real source of the human race – 'The last Adam is indeed the first; as he himself says: "I am the first and the last"' (359). The Catechism's claim, in the very next line, that the human race forms a unity 'because of its common origin' (360) would therefore seem to found 'the law of human solidarity and charity' not on a mere common genetic origin, but on the unity of humanity in its Redeemer.

Human beings, created in the image of God, straddle both heaven and earth, for they are 'at once corporeal and spiritual'. Recognizing that it is in our spiritual principle, our innermost life, that we most closely reflect God, the Catechism nevertheless affirms the profound unity of body and soul, 'not two natures united, but rather ... a single nature'. The material, bodily life of humanity therefore takes on its own dignity as part of the image of God – a notion with wide-ranging implications for our attitudes towards the material well-being of all our human brothers and sisters.

The Catechism's teaching on gender is concerned to emphasize both the equality and the complementarity of the sexes. Maleness and femaleness are realities which are 'good, and willed by God'. Men and women each possess an inalienable and equal dignity which comes directly from God. The 'particular perfections' of men and women reflect realities in the mystery of God himself, who is neither male nor female but in whom are realities corresponding to the 'perfections' of each sex, such as motherhood or fatherhood. Men and women are made for each other, not because either sex is in itself half-made or incomplete, but because like their creator, Father, Son and Holy Spirit, they are made for the loving communion of equal persons. Together they transmit the gift of life, and together they exercise a stewardship over creation which is not 'an arbitrary and destructive domination', but a loving exercise of God's providence towards all that he has made.

Paradise – and Fall (374–384, 385–421)

With the Catechism's discussion of the state of humanity in Paradise, and the story of the Fall, we come hard up against the problematic nature of the Catechism's use of Scripture, and its mediation of Catholic tradition on these issues. At the heart of the Christian gospel is the certainty that human beings were meant for God, and for human flourishing. Yet we experience in ourselves and in our shared history the reality of alienation, we find ourselves at odds with ourselves and at enmity with our neighbour, subject to disease, death, poverty and chance. We die, as all the animals die, yet a special horror attaches to our dying. We alone experience our mortality, not simply as the natural end of bodily existence, but as what the dying man in *The Dream of Gerontius* calls 'the masterful negation and collapse of all that makes me man'. For us, death is the sacrament of our alienation from ourselves and our world.

That alienation pervades all we do and are. We are driven by longings and appetites which cloud our judgements and complicate our actions. We see what is good, and we fail to do it. These ills are written large in the history of society and culture: war, domination, oppression seem to be the energies which again and again erupt into human history and distort and destroy the communities we live in. All of us can see that there is something profoundly amiss, all of us can see how we ought to behave. We know that it might be otherwise, we know ourselves not merely as victims but as sinners, responsible for the evil acts we perform, and yet we know also that the spiral of evil and frustration within which we live is not something we or anyone else can simply 'snap out of'. We know we cannot be good, or happy, simply by trying harder.

This much all human beings can see. For believers in the God who creates and redeems, the horror and puzzle of sin is particularly acute. This world and all that is in it comes from the hand of God: he made it, and found it good, he loves it and us with a father's, with a mother's, love. And yet we, his children, are cut off from his presence, at odds with his will, deprived of his blessings.

The opening chapters of the book of Genesis explore these contradictions in the form of myth, the story of how it was 'in the beginning'. 'Myth' in our culture is often taken as a term of abuse – a false tale, a fairy story, the opposite of 'truth'. In the ancient world, however, myth meant something quite different, archetypal stories which convey truths we can live – and die – by. Myths were often the way in which truths too deep for reasoning were expressed, and every culture still retains these foundational myths, which shape our thinking about ourselves and the world we live in. The Genesis stories are myth in this deeper and older sense.

And so Genesis imagines the origins of the human race in the archetypal Good Place, a garden 'in Eden, in the East'. From this garden flow out the four great rivers which brought life and renewal to the world of the Middle East in biblical times, and in this garden God set Man and Woman, at peace with him, with themselves and with the beasts. They were

vegetarian, they were innocent, they were without the artifi-
ciality of developed society. Eden is the place not only of
innocence, but of order, it is where Adam names the creatures, 'and whatever the man called every living creature, that
was its name'. As in a fairy story, God, who walks with them in
the cool of the evening, gives them the free run of this
Paradise, where everything is good to eat, but he forbids them
to eat from a particular tree. Tempted by the wily serpent, the
woman eats and gives her mate to eat also: and so God casts
them out from Paradise, and sets a guard on the gate. From
now on the earth would be cursed to them, and they would
have to wrest their food from thorns and briars, from now on
child-bearing would be painful and dangerous. And in a final
mythic touch, God condemns the serpent to slither on its
belly and to be hated by all. And so the story sets out the
agonizing contradictions which we all feel in our hearts – that
we are made for glory yet live in sorrow; that God is our
Father yet we flee from his face; that life, which is the breath
of God, for us begins with a cry and ends in death.

Is this a story about long ago and far away, or about the
here and now, about how we find it is with us? Was there a first
pair, full of grace, in harmony with God, and is our present
state of alienation, even our bondage to death, the result of
an historical event, some action of our forefather and mother
in the mists of time? When we talk of 'original sin', do we
describe, as the Catechism says we do 'a primeval event, a
deed that took place at the beginning of the history of
man'?

There is of course no doubt that till this century the
overwhelming majority of Christians would not have ques-
tioned that this was indeed the case. But in the light of what
we now know about the date, composition and literary character of the Genesis stories, and in the light of the growing
complexity of the story of human origins as they are revealed
by genetics, palaeontology and archaeology, we can hardly
still maintain the literal truth of these profound stories. Can
we seriously say, for example, as the Catechism does, but the
book of Genesis does not, that before the Fall our ancestors

'would not have to suffer or to die'? In the fourth century St Athanasius pointed out that whatever else the text of Genesis meant, it did not mean that natural mortality was the consequence of sin: for him the 'death' which followed sin was eternal, not temporal, death.[15]

What Athanasius realized so long ago, we too know for certain. The bones of the dinosaurs and of the early ancestors of the human race remain in the earth to tell us that this is not so. We do not die because Adam sinned, we die because we are animals, because our bodies are part of the natural world in which growth and flourishing and decay are part of the created order. Most Catholics in the West at any rate would now accept that some version of the theory of evolution is likely to be true, that the human species like the other animals emerged over immensities of time from more primitive forms of life. This conviction does have far-reaching implications for theology, since the energies and characteristics which seem to underly the success of particular species in the evolutionary process – the ability to compete with and in the long-run defeat weaker groups – seem perilously close to the energies we associate with sinfulness. This sense of nature 'red in tooth and claw' seems to have posed a particular threat to the faith of Christians in the nineteenth century, and remains part of the enigma of evil and suffering for all believers. In the twentieth century the need to integrate a belief in creation with what science suggests about the biological origins of the human race has been strongly felt by Christian thinkers. The Jesuit Teilhard de Chardin for example offered an account of the emergence of the human species in evolutionary terms in which suffering and evil were necessary parts of the maturing of creation, but his account makes little apparent sense of traditional Christian ways of thinking and talking about sin. Teilhard's suggested solutions to these problems probably fail in the end, but he at least recognized that our current scientific knowledge does affect the way we can read the Genesis narratives of the Fall. However we resolve these problems, this is an issue no adult catechesis can afford to neglect, though little help will be found in this Catechism.

This is not to say that the Genesis stories are 'untrue'. They touch truths so deep and so universal that simply to read them is to feel a pang of recognition, and with it something of the sorrow of humanity at odds with God, itself and the world. What the stories – and the Church's centuries of reflection on these stories – speak of are realities which we all can test for ourselves. We know that simply by virtue of being born as human beings we are caught up in a spiral of evil which, of our own strength, we cannot escape. In part this is to do with the sinful structures of society (and the book of Genesis uses other stories, like the myth of Babel, to explore the social dimension of human sinfulness). But we also know that no mere social restructuring will straighten our twisted hearts: the Irish poet W. B. Yeats caught this point nicely in a jingle:

> Hurrah for Revolution, and more cannon shot!
> A beggar upon horseback lashes a beggar on foot:
> Hurrah for revolution and cannon come again:
> The beggars have changed places, but the lash goes on.[16]

And we feel that it should not be so, that humanity deserves better and was meant for better. We sense our greatness, the freedom of the children of God, but we experience our enslavement. The stories in Genesis enshrine these profound truths by projecting them into the unimaginably remote past – long ago and far away, in the beginning. So we cannot do without these stories, but we must not take them for what they are not meant to be, histories. If the world is to hear the message these stories contain, it is the task of catechesis to explain their real content, and not to be satisfied, as the authors of the Catechism seem to be, with repeating the picture-language of the tradition. What was plausible cosmology to St Augustine in the fifth century, when the details of our understanding of original sin were being worked out, will not now serve as literal truth.

Nor does it need to, for the essence of the doctrine of original sin as an observable fact, and not merely some ancient legend in which snakes talk and men feel no shame, is well-expressed by Cardinal Newman, in a famous passage from his *Apologia pro Vita Sua*:

> If I looked into a mirror, and did not see my face, I should have the sort of feeling which actually comes upon me, when I look into this living busy world, and see no reflexion of its Creator ... to consider the world in its length and breadth, its various history, the many races of man, their starts, their fortunes, their mutual alienation, their conflicts ... their aimless courses, their random achievements and acquirements, ... the greatness and littleness of man, his far-reaching aims, his short duration, the curtain hung over his futurity, the disappointments of life, the defeat of good, the success of evil, physical pain, mental anguish, the prevalence and intensity of sin, the pervading idolatries, the corruptions, the dreary hopeless irreligion, that condition of the whole race, so fearfully yet exactly described in the Apostle's words, 'having no hope and without God in the world' ...
>
> What shall be said to this heart-piercing, reason-bewildering fact? I can only answer, that either there is no Creator, or this living society of men is in a true sense discarded from his presence ... If there be a God, since there is a God, the human race is implicated in some terrible aboriginal calamity. It is out of joint with the purposes of its Creator. This is a fact, a fact as true as the fact of its existence; and thus the doctrine of what is theologically called original sin becomes to me almost as certain as that the world exists, and as the existence of God.[17]

In considering the Catechism's teaching on all this, it is once again worth noticing the far greater care which was taken over the drafting of the passage on original sin in the Second Vatican Council's Pastoral Constitution on the Church in the Modern World, *Gaudium et Spes*. The Catechism declares that the Fall was 'a primeval event, a deed that took place at the beginning of the history of man', and as its authority for this claim, cites *Gaudium et Spes* 13.1. What this paragraph actually says is that 'Although set by God in a state of rectitude, man, enticed by the evil one, abused his freedom at the very start of history'. This is a considerably more general formula, which need not necessarily involve the notion of original sin proceeding from a single historical 'deed' by an individual ancestor of the rest of humanity, and *Gaudium et Spes* at once proceeds to locate the doctrine in terms of our own experience.

> What Revelation makes known to us is confirmed by our own experience. For when man looks into his own heart he finds that he is drawn towards what is wrong and sunk in many evils which cannot come from his good creator ... Man is therefore divided in himself ...

And the Catechism itself firmly locates the meaning and application of all this in the revelation of God in Jesus Christ. Christ reveals both grace and sin: as we recognize in him our Redeemer and see the depth of God's love for us, we grasp also the measure of our alienation from God. The crucifixion of Christ reveals the fate of love and truth in our fallen world, and in it sin is revealed, judged and forgiven (388). The story of Adam and Eve does not point us backwards, to a remote event in whose consequences we are somehow inexplicably caught up, like the hapless child who inherits from its parents some hereditary blood disease. It points us forward, to our destiny in Christ, God's loving answer to the mystery of sin and suffering and despair. The Garden of Eden stands at the end of our history, as much as at its beginning. So the doctrine of original sin is, paradoxically, *good news*: in Paul's words, 'Where sin increased, grace abounded all the more'. In the gift of his Son to heal our sin God gives the world a gift more precious than anything it lacked. And so just as it began its exposition of creation with the readings from the Easter Vigil, the Catechism concludes its treatment of creation and Fall in the joyful words of the Easter Exsultet, the Church's ecstatic hymn to the risen Light of Christ –

> *O felix culpa*, O happy fault, O truly necessary sin of Adam, which gained for us so great a Redeemer. (412)

NOTES

1 *A New Catechism: Catholic Faith for Adults* (New York and London: Herder and Herder, 1967).
2 *Dei Verbum* 2.
3 Para. 27, quoting from *Gaudium et Spes* 19.
4 St Augustine, *Commentary on John: Patrologia Latina* 35, 1631; quoted in Nicholas Lash, *Believing Three Ways in One God* (London, 1992), p. 126.
5 2 Corinthians 1:19–20.
6 See the ecumenical edition and commentary edited by J. L. Houlden, *The Interpretation of the Bible in the Church* (London, 1995).
7 I borrow this rendering from Robert Murray SJ in *Commentary on the Catechism of the Catholic Church*, ed. M. J. Walsh (London, 1994), p. 25.
8 Karl Rahner, *Theological Investigations* VI (London and Baltimore, 1969), pp. 390–8, and his discussion of Catholic responses to his suggestion in *Theological Investigations* XIV (London, 1976), pp. 280–94.
9 *Dei Verbum* 7–8.
10 Exodus 3:1–15.
11 See for example John E. Huesman SJ in R. Brown *et al.* (eds), *The Jerome Bible Commentary* (London, 1984), p. 50.
12 Isaiah 6:5.
13 Dante, *Paradiso*, canto xxxiii, line 145.
14 Isaiah 51:9–16; 48:12–16; 55:10–11.
15 'if they transgressed and turned away and became evil, they should know that they would suffer that corruption in death which was natural to them ... for to "die in death" [Genesis 2:16] surely means just this, not merely to die, but to remain in the corruption of death': Athanasius, *De Incarnatione* 3; translation from Henry Bettenson, *The Early Christian Fathers* (London, 1956), p. 378.
16 'The Great Day' in *The Collected Poems of W. B. Yeats*, ed. A. Norman Jeffares (London, 1989), p. 430.
17 J. H. Newman, *Apologia Pro Vita Sua* (London, 1898), pp. 241–3.

PART TWO

I believe in Jesus Christ, the only Son of God

AT THE HEART of the Gospel is a person. In Jesus Christ the mystery of God is made plain, or rather, it is made flesh. In this man, in all that he did and said, all that he was and is, the eternal, unknowable God is revealed. Because Jesus called him Abba, Father, we can say to the Lord of the universe 'Our Father', because Jesus died a criminal's death, rejected by all, we know that an utter self-giving love, which holds nothing back, underlies the whole of creation. Christ, in Pascal's words, is the centre towards which all things tend, the key to the mystery of existence. Catholic faith, therefore, is not primarily knowledge of a set of doctrines, but trust in a specific human being who, we believe, perfectly and completely embodies and reveals the eternal God. 'At the heart of catechesis we find . . . a Person, . . . Jesus of Nazareth, the only Son from the Father' (426). At the beginning of our century, the great theologian Friedrich von Hügel expressed the inexhaustible richness and centrality of Jesus Christ for all who believe, and for the history of the human race.

> A person came, and lived, and loved, and did and taught, and
> died and rose again, and lives on by his power and his spirit
> for ever within us and amongst us, so unspeakably rich and yet
> so simple, so sublime and yet so homely, so divinely above us
> in being so divinely near – that his character and teaching
> require, for an ever fuller yet never complete understanding,
> the varying study, and different experiments and applications,
> embodiments and unrolling of all the races and civilisations, of
> all the individual and corporate, the simultaneous and

successive experiences of the human race until the end of time.[1]

And so the second section of the Catechism opens with a solemn declaration of faith in this person, in all his human particularity.

> We believe and confess that Jesus of Nazareth, born a Jew of a daughter of Israel at Bethlehem at the time of King Herod the Great and the emperor Caesar Augustus, a carpenter by trade, who died in Jerusalem under the procurator Pontius Pilate during the reign of the emperor Tiberius, is the eternal Son of God made man. (423)

In fact, this resounding declaration of faith in Christ's divinity colours all that follows in this section, and anyone using this part of the Catechism needs to be aware of the distinctive character of its presentation of the mystery of God in Christ. Throughout its treatment of the second article of the Creed, the Catechism employs a 'descending Christology', which emphasizes the divine origins and nature of Christ as the Incarnate Second Person of the Trinity, and expounds his earthly actions always in that light. At one level this is a completely scriptural and patristic emphasis, which hardly merits comment. From the beginning of the Christian proclamation the Church confessed Jesus' unique relationship of Sonship to the Father, and saw his mission in terms of divine self-humbling: for St Paul the movement of divine love in the life and death of Jesus was one of descent, from bliss to suffering, from glory to humiliation, from life to death.

> Christ Jesus . . . though he was in the form of God, did not count equality with God a thing to be grasped, but emptied himself, taking the form of a servant, being born in the likeness of men. And being found in human form he humbled himself and became obedient unto death, even death on a cross. (Philippians 2:5–9)

That 'self-emptying' of Christ (the Greek word is *kenōsis*) became a favourite theme in the writings of the early Church Fathers, who loved to dwell on the divine compassion, which caused the eternal Word of God to cast himself down into our suffering and mortal condition, so that he might lift us up to share the life of God himself.[2] But we need to remind ourselves that although this great truth was at the heart of the Gospel from the very beginning, its full implications were only slowly and painfully teased out: it was to take the Church centuries to formulate its belief in the divinity of Christ. Even more crucially, we need to grasp that for the first generation of Christians, for the apostles themselves, the full confession of who Christ was came *after* the Resurrection. The events of Easter revealed the real meaning of the life and death of the man they had spoken with, trudged the roads of Judaea with, broken bread with, and, from a distance, watched bleed to death in agony. The breathtaking folly of the Gospel comes precisely from its identification of a real flesh-and-blood human being, a man who went hungry, needed to learn things, shared the (sometimes mistaken) beliefs of his contemporaries and, at the last, was arrested and executed, with the eternal Word and Wisdom and Glory and Power of God himself. One of the problems of the Catechism's handling of this, the greatest truth of our faith, is that it sometimes moves too quickly to the divine dimension of Christ's life and sayings, without giving due weight to their human character. As we shall see, the Catechism systematically tends to underplay the element of struggle, suffering, temptation and limitation in the life of Jesus. While acknowledging this aspect of the Incarnation, it often hurries past it, and so at times leaves us with a Christ who seems to share little of the bewilderment and pain of our existence. We are all familiar with pious pictures of Christ as a handsome, white, well-groomed athlete whose head is encased in a helmet of light, a hero who, one feels, would triumph effortlessly over his enemies. Knowledge of Christ's divinity can be a temptation to empty his humanity of its reality, and that tendency in the Christian tradition has helped drive good men and women away from a Christ they cannot identify with, because they cannot believe that he has identified with them. Stevie Smith speaks for all such people in her poem 'Was He Married?'

Was he married, did he try
To support as he grew less fond of them
Wife and family?

No,
He never suffered such a blow.

Did he feel pointless, feeble and distrait,
Unwanted by everyone and in the way?

From his cradle he was purposeful,
His bent strong and his mind full.

Did he love people very much
Yet find them die one day?

He did not love in the human way.

Did he ask how long it would go on,
Wonder if Death could be counted on for an end?

He did not feel like this,
He had a future of bliss.

Did he feel strong
Pain for being wrong?

He was not wrong, he was right,
He suffered from others', not his own, spite.

But there is no suffering like having made a mistake
Because of being of an inferior make.

He was not inferior,
He was superior . . .

All human beings should have a medal,
A god cannot carry it, he is not able . . .[3]

This, of course, is a parody of what Christians actually
believe about the God who has declared that 'my power is
made perfect in weakness' (2 Corinthians 12:9), and whose
strength to save was revealed in the utter defeat of the Cross,
but it touches a nerve all the same. In catechesis especially,
where we are dealing with people's uncertainties, and their
reaching out to faith, it is important to recognize that the
Church's faith itself grew and developed, that the gospels
show us the apostles themselves struggling to come to terms

with the mystery of Christ. The nineteenth-century Danish philosopher Søren Kierkegaard described the bewildered disciples after the Resurrection asking 'Who was that? What was that?' Each Christian generation is confronted afresh with those questions, and there is a danger of superficiality in moving too quickly and too easily to the 'right' answers. In our own generation many Christians have found inspiration and help in an understanding of Christ which starts not from above, from the serene truth of his divinity, but from below, from close attention to and identification with what the gospels tell us of his humanity, of the specific circumstances in which he lived and preached, and of the dimension of struggle and limitation which humanity entails. The Catechism's handling of the gospels seldom touches on the historical particularity of Jesus' life and times, focusing instead on a more spiritual or doctrinal reading of Scripture. In this it perhaps seeks to offer a corrective to such human-centred Christologies, which can reduce Christ to little more than a hero-figure or role-model. As we shall see, however; there is a price to pay for its consistent emphasis on Christ's transcendent divinity.

The name and titles of Christ (430–455)

The Catechism begins its treatment of the Incarnation and Redemption with a discussion of the name and titles of Christ as they are set out in the Creed – 'And in *Jesus Christ*, his only *Son*, our *Lord*'. The interpretation it offers of these names and titles well demonstrates the Catechism's emphasis on a 'descending Christology' in which Christ's eternal nature is the main concern, and its tendency to 'read back' developed doctrine into the New Testament sources.

The name Jesus, for example, 'God saves', is the same as Joshua, and was common in our Lord's time. Yet it is explained here as essentially asserting Christ's divinity. It is, according to the Catechism, equivalent to the divine Name, 'the name of the Saviour God ... invoked only once in the year by the high priest in atonement for the sins of Israel'

(433). Citing Philippians 2:9–10, the Catechism identifies the name 'Jesus' as the 'name which is above every name' – though in fact Paul here is referring to the title 'Lord' which God has given the risen Christ. All this is to make the name Jesus carry a very heavy theological weight, the fruit of later piety rather than the explicit intention of the New Testament writers. There is nothing wrong with this procedure in itself, of course. The name 'Jesus' does in fact contain the letters of the Hebrew name for God, the 'Tetragrammaton' YHWH, and, as the Catechism rightly points out, Christians have always reverenced the Holy Name of Jesus, invoking it against evil, and placing it at the centre of their prayers. But the whole point of invoking a human name as the very name of God, of replacing YHWH with Jesus, is that in doing so we highlight the wonderful mercy of God in the Incarnation. He is no longer to be found in the burning bush, or hidden in the holy of holies where only the high priest may utter his Name: he has drawn near to us, and is to be found in one of ourselves, in a man. As Cardinal Joseph Ratzinger has put it, 'The Name is no longer merely a word but a person: Jesus himself'.[4] The Church has always known this, and in the medieval West, at any rate, the name of Jesus was the focus for devotion to Christ's *humanity*, rather than to his divinity . The 'sweet' and 'good' name of Jesus, invoked in countless medieval prayers, was the symbol of Christ's human closeness to us, not of his transcendent Godhead – as the popular fourteenth-century devotional writer Ludolf the Carthusian wrote:

> O good Jesus . . . how is it that you are sweeter in the heart of one who loves you in the form of flesh than as the Word, sweeter in a way which is humble than in that which is exalted . . . it is sweeter to see you as a man bearing every aspect of human nature to the end, than as God manifesting divine nature, to see you as the dying Redeemer than as the invisible Creator.[5]

Christology from the 'bottom up' is not a modern invention!

In the same way the Catechism sees the title 'Christ' or Messiah, meaning the Anointed One, as revealing the Lord's eternal nature (436–440). Explaining the place of the title Messiah in Israel's hopes for a fulfilment of the promises to David of an everlasting Kingdom, the Catechism nevertheless sees Peter's proclamation of Jesus as Messiah at Pentecost as going beyond this to a recognition of the 'transcendent identity' of the divine Son of Man. This is doubtless true enough, but at Pentecost Peter specifically declares that 'God has *made him* both Lord and Christ, this Jesus whom you crucified' (Acts 2:36), a clear indication that he was thinking in terms of the exaltation of Jesus at the Resurrection, rather than of his eternal nature as the Word. Once again the biblical material is being nudged in the direction of sub-sequent doctrinal development, and the apostles are being credited with language and thought-patterns which belong to a later stage of Christian reflection and confession, and to a different cultural context.

The same tendency to collapse together different strands in the tradition can be seen in the Catechism's explanation of the title *Son of God*. In St John's gospel this title clearly does signify a developed theology of Christ's divine nature, and a claim to identity with God. But in the gospels of Matthew, Mark, and Luke the matter is more complicated. There the title is probably equivalent to 'Messiah', in the Catechism's words 'a less than divine title'. So Peter's confession at Caesarea that 'you are the Christ, the Son of the Living God' does not necessarily represent a full awareness of Christ's divinity, and indeed many Catholic commentators believe that this story is displaced in the gospels, and is the product of the Church's post-Resurrection faith rather than the life-time of Jesus. The disciples from the first certainly grasped that Jesus claimed and enjoyed a uniquely intimate relation-ship with the Father: but it would take the outpouring of the Holy Spirit and the prayer, reflection and experience of generations to discover the full implications of that inti-macy.

The Catechism is on firmer ground in seeing in the use of the title 'Lord' (*Kurios* in Greek) for the risen Jesus an affirmation that 'the power, honour and glory due to God the Father are due also to Jesus' (446–451). It also helpfully draws attention to the far-reaching political and moral implications of the confession that *Jesus is Lord*. To name him Lord was not merely to accept the notion of his divinity, but in the process to reject all idolatries, to recognize that no-one should submit their 'personal freedom in an absolute manner to any earthly power, but only to God the Father and the Lord Jesus Christ'. Christian faith has profound consequences for our attitude to all the forces and 'isms' which assert claims over or attempt to enslave human beings – political, social, national, even religious claims. To confess that Jesus is Lord is to proclaim liberty to captives, to find the 'centre and purpose' of human history in him and in the freedom he brings (450).

HE WAS CONCEIVED BY THE POWER OF THE HOLY SPIRIT, AND BORN OF THE VIRGIN MARY

With its consideration of the nature of the Incarnation, the Catechism moves to the 'distinctive sign of Christian faith', the very nub of Catholic belief, the appearance in human nature, in our flesh, of God himself –

> eternity contracted to a span,
> our God incomprehensibly made man.

It begins by asking 'Why did the Word become flesh?', a question which receives a full answer only in the later section on the role of the Cross in the Paschal mystery (599–618). But from the very outset of its discussion of the Incarnation the Catechism sets Christ's birth in the context of Calvary. He came into the world, as the Creed says, '*propter nos homines, et propter nostram salutem*', 'for us men, and for our salvation', 'to save us by reconciling us with God' (457). This particular answer was not inevitable. In the Middle Ages, scholastic theologians hotly debated the reasons for the Incarnation. Some, following St Thomas, believed that Christ took our human nature essentially because of the Fall, as God's remedy for our sin. Others, following Duns Scotus, argued that even had humankind never sinned, the Word of God would still have taken flesh, to exalt human nature and complete his Image in us. The Catechism incorporates elements of both perceptions, teaching that Christ came into the world not merely to save us from our sins, but to reveal God's love, to be a model of holiness, and to make us partakers of the divine nature (458–460). Yet in all this the emphasis remains on the compassionate concern of God to raise up his fallen creatures, to rescue us from sin. The descent from heaven to the stable at Bethlehem has its natural completion on the Cross, in the garden tomb, indeed in the very pit of hell itself, into which Christ, 'for us and for our salvation', did not hesitate to descend. For the Catechism, the theology of Incarnation is firmly tied to the Easter mystery of death and resurrection. We shall see the importance of this emphasis when we come to consider its teaching on the death of Christ.

True God and true man

For every generation of Christians, the confession that Jesus of Nazareth was both truly human and the eternal Word of God, the second person of the Blessed Trinity, has seemed both absolutely necessary, and totally beyond our comprehension. Catholic Christianity has found no other way of doing justice to its profoundest belief, that in the life and death of this man we see revealed not just a picture of what God is *like*, but, in the words of Newman's hymn, 'God's presence, and his very self, and essence all Divine'. In modern times Christians wrestling with this belief have been tempted to soften or even to abandon the notion of the divinity of Jesus. Oddly, to our perceptions, the Christians of the early centuries of the Church were tempted in precisely the opposite direction, to doubt his true humanity. The Catechism's section 'True God and true man' offers a potted history of the early Christological debates, which seems too compressed and selective to be likely to attract many enthusiastic readers (464–469), but which does serve to remind us of the evolving character of the Church's faith in this great mystery. The Catechism quotes at length from the definition of the Council of Chalcedon, which set out in the fifth century the terms in which Catholics ever since have proclaimed the truth of the Incarnation. The bishops and theologians assembled at Chalcedon insisted that Christ was in no sense a mixture of the human and divine, some sort of spiritual amphibian, half man, half God. His divine nature was not changed by the assumption of human nature, and though human nature was infinitely ennobled by being gathered up into the Godhead, it was not absorbed or annihilated. Jesus was indeed the Son of God, but he was also fully and perfectly human, like us in every respect, except for sin (467).

The importance of this truth for Christian faith cannot be overestimated. Because of our faith in the Incarnation, we know that a human being, possessing all the faculties that we have, and possessing *only* the faculties that we have, perfectly loved and perfectly obeyed God, and was the perfect instrument of God's love in and for the world. A human being, one of us, redeemed the human race. Christians know this to be true, yet they have repeatedly and with the best of intentions tried to soften its implications. Theologians and preachers have emphasized the superiority of Jesus' human nature, and have hinted that after all the union of the divine and human natures in Jesus *must* have blurred the distinction between them. So it has been thought that the human mind of Jesus shared in the eternal wisdom and omniscience of the Word of God, and passages in the Scriptures where Jesus expresses ignorance – for example about the timing of the end of the world – have been explained away . It has been taught, by St

Thomas among others, that from the first moment of his existence to the moment of his death, Christ enjoyed the beatific vision, seeing God face to face. This has been squared with his human frailty and suffering by supposing that his mind operated on a series of levels, and that at the highest level he enjoyed the beatific vision, while on the lower slopes he suffered pain, puzzlement and loss. These speculations were devised to meet real difficulties, and we should think twice before dismissing them out of hand. We cannot know or imagine what it must be for a human mind to be united to the eternal Word and Wisdom of God. Yet they smack of unreality, and threaten to reduce our belief in the real humanity of Jesus to a sham. The Catechism, as one might expect from its strong emphasis on a 'descending Christo-logy', is itself in danger of falling into this trap. It accepts that Christ had a human soul and mind, and that therefore his knowledge 'could not in itself be unlimited' – but it qualifies this by drawing on patristic teaching that nevertheless Christ's human nature 'not by itself but by its union with the Word, knew and showed forth in itself everything that per-tains to God'. So Christ 'enjoyed in his human knowledge the fullness of understanding of the eternal plans he had come to reveal' (472–473). If this means that Jesus knew and under-stood all that he needed to do to accomplish the work God sent him to achieve, it is of course obviously true. More seems to be implied, however, that Jesus 'really' knew all that the Word knew. So the Catechism declares that during his life, his agony and his Passion, 'Jesus knew and loved us each and all'. This is a favourite theme for sermons and pious medita-tions, but as a literal proposition it is clearly problematic: to know each and every one of the billions of human beings, past, present and to come, is a clear human impossibility which no finite mind could encompass (478). Such inflated claims about Jesus' human mind threaten the doctrine of the Incarnation just as much as do doubts about his divinity. We will see the same reluctance to confront the scandal of the Incarnation much more sharply focused in the Catechism's extremely gingerly handling of Christ's anguish in Gethsemane (612).

Born of the Virgin Mary

At this point in its discussion of the Incarnation, the Catechism turns to the role of the Virgin Mary. Emphasizing that the Church speaks of Mary in order to speak more clearly of Christ (487) the Catechism locates the role and privileges of Mary within the work of the Incarnation. She is the culmination of a process of preparation seen at work in the holy women of the Old Testament, and she is the representative of the faithful remnant of Israel, who waited in hope for the promised Messiah: in the words of the Council's great Constitution on the Church, *Lumen Gentium*, Mary

> stands out among the poor and humble of the Lord, who confidently hope for and receive salvation from him. After a long period of waiting the times are fulfilled in her, the exalted Daughter of Sion, and the new plan of salvation is established. (489, quoting *Lumen Gentium* 55)

So all that we say of Mary is related to her role as the Mother of the Saviour, her privileges too are part of the *propter nos*, 'for us', of God's self-gift in the Incarnation. Her sinlessness is not a gift for her sole benefit, but God's way of removing the barrier of sin which might have led her to refuse the obedience of faith at the Annunciation. Her virginity serves to emphasize the initiative of God in sending his Son, whose coming into the world was 'not of blood nor of the will of the flesh, nor of the will of man, but of God', a sign of a new beginning for the human race, the new birth, and a sign of Mary's integrity in faith, her absolute obedience to her Lord and ours. She is thus 'the symbol and the most perfect realization of the Church' which, like her, hears the word of faith and brings forth sons and daughters by the power of the Holy Spirit, and which, like Mary, is virginal in keeping pure and entire the faith of Christ (503–507).

In all this the Catechism echoes the teaching of the Second Vatican Council. One of the Council's most momentous steps was the decision not to issue a separate document on the place of Mary, as many of the Council Fathers wished to do, but to incorporate what it had to say about her as the final chapter of the constitution on the Church, *Lumen Gentium.* This apparently small gesture had the effect of placing Mary back within the context of the Church, among her fellow Christians, and not over against them or above them, as had been the tendency of much post-Reformation devotion to her. The Council, and the Catechism, emphasize that Mary too is one of the redeemed, our representative. Her 'yes' to God is spoken for us –'in the name of all human nature', as St Thomas says (511). We too, like her, must in our turn become Mothers of God, by faith and the power of the Spirit bringing Christ to birth in our hearts and in a world that still does not know but more than ever desperately needs him.

The mysteries of Christ's life (512–570)

Unlike the gospels, but like St Paul, the creeds tell us nothing about the life of Christ. Though the pattern of the Creed is a sort of story – he was 'conceived, born, suffered, died, rose, ascended, will come again', that story moves at once from the birth of Christ to his crucifixion, passing over in silence all that he did and said. Yet the life-story of Jesus matters to Christians, because we believe that the timeless God (for 'timeless' is what eternal means) has appeared in time, and has shown himself for who and what he is, in the life and deeds and sayings of a Jew in first-century Palestine. In the light of Christmas and Easter, all the events of Christ's life can be seen to be charged with saving significance. By his poverty he enriches us, by his submission and obedience he atones for our rebellion, by his healings and exorcisms he takes on our infirmities and bears our diseases (517). So the longest single section of the Catechism's treatment of the Incarna-tion, fifty paragraphs of it, is devoted to an exposition of what it calls 'The mysteries of Christ's life'. This terminology for the actions and teaching of Christ may at first sight puzzle some readers. It will be familiar to readers of St Ignatius

Loyola's *Spiritual Exercises,* but here seems to derive from a
now almost forgotten but once classic theological work of the
1920s by the Benedictine Dom Columba Marmion, *Christ in
His Mysteries,*[6] and the Catechism refers us to the writings of
the seventeenth-century French priest St John Eudes, who
made use of the same notion.[7] The essential point is that the
life and words of Christ are *sacramental* in character – 'mystery' is simply the Greek word translated by the Latin *sacra-
mentum.* A sacrament is the outward sign of an inner reality,
something which at one and the same time shows and communicates some hidden truth or power. So all that Christ says
and does reveals and communicates some aspect of his saving
work. The *propter nos,* 'for us, and for our salvation', of the
Incarnation means that all that he did was for our sake.
United to us in our humanity, he gives us a claim on all that
he has as the Son of God. In part this sharing comes by
imitation, when we follow him as our model (520), but much
more profoundly we share in these realities by our participation in the life, prayer and worship of the Church, above all
by the sacramental celebrations in which the Easter mysteries
are recalled and renewed for us. The life and ministry of
Christ are not simply historical events in the distant past, but
the movement of humanity towards God, into which we can
and must be drawn as sharers, not as spectators.

A fundamental part of the Catechism's teaching at this
point is the notion of the Incarnation as a 'recapitulation' or
summing up in Christ's life of all that we have and are and
suffer. By entering into every aspect of the human situation,
Christ fills every human activity and experience with his
saving presence. So the Catechism quotes St Irenaeus, with
whom this teaching is specially associated:

> For this reason Christ experienced all the stages of life,
> thereby giving communion with God to all men. (518)

This notion of recapitulation is an enormously rich and
potentially very helpful one, and it recurs again and again in
the Catechism in a variety of forms. It is ultimately rooted not
only in Paul's teaching about the first and the second Adam,

but also in the epistle to the Hebrews, with its teaching about Christ as a high priest 'able to sympathize with our weaknesses' because he has been tempted 'in every respect as we are' (Hebrews 4:14–16). But it has its problems. How all-inclusive is this process of 'recapitulation' in Christ? He was male, not female, young, not old, single, not married. In what sense does he enter into the whole of human experience? This issue has been sharpened by recent official teaching on the exclusion of women from the ordained ministry of the Church. If Jesus' maleness is in some way fundamental to the sacramental continuation of his work in the Church, where does femaleness fit in the process of 'recapitulation'? For Irenaeus and the early Fathers and medieval Scholastics this was not an issue, for they shared the (mistaken) medical beliefs of their day that male human beings were the complete item, and that femaleness consisted in the lack of certain physical characteristics: thus maleness *included* femaleness. By becoming male, Christ included in himself *all* that was human. No-one now seriously maintains this way of thinking about gender, yet the grounds given for the exclusion of women from the priesthood seem to attribute salvific and sacramental significance specifically to Christ's maleness, and hence that of his ministers. How then are women saved? Attempts to use this part of the Catechism, and to explore the rich notion of 'recapitulation' it depends on, will need to confront such issues with imagination, sensitivity and tact.

The handling of the 'mysteries of Christ's life' also highlights another feature of the Catechism's approach to Scripture which is linked to its 'descending Christology', but which many people may regret. A consistent feature of much modern New Testament scholarship has been its 'quest for the historical Jesus', the search to discover in the gospels the specific facts and circumstances of Jesus' life, and his place in the society of first-century Palestine. This 'quest' has sometimes been pursued with the idea of driving a wedge between what the Church preaches and believes about Jesus, and the 'real' man, but the attempt to place Jesus more firmly in his

historical context has also been taken up by devout Christians, eager to explore more deeply the meaning of the
Incarnation for the first disciples and for us. The eternal
Word of God did not become human in some merely general
sense: he became a Jewish man of first-century Palestine.
Every detail of that life is therefore full of significance. The
Catechism itself declares that catechesis should 'make use of
all the richness of the mysteries of Jesus' (513). For many
modern theologians, this means a careful attention to the
fine detail of Christ's life as far as they can be reconstructed
using all the techniques of scholarship at our disposal. Only
in this way can we avoid pious generalities which mask the
challenge of the real Christ. While accepting the traditional
doctrines about Christ, these theologians have called for a
continuing engagement with the problem of Christology, the
question of who Jesus is for us, a question which can only be
answered by obedient attention to what the gospels tell us of
him.

This point of view has been particularly important for
liberation theologians, who have sought to reconstruct the
precise nature of Christ's preaching to and about the poor.
Who were these poor? On the answer to that question will
turn our understanding of the Beatitudes, and so our understanding of who the kingdom of heaven belongs to. Only if we
consider the attitudes and actions of Jesus to his own society,
even to the politics of that society, can we discover where he
is to be found in our own. Christology must start from
below.[8]

We will find none of this in the Catechism's handling of the
life of Jesus. Though it is attentive to Scripture, there is little
engagement with these sorts of methods and questions, and
the flood of work on the background to the New Testament
which has transformed our picture of the Judaism within
which the Lord preached, and the society to which he addressed his message, has left little trace in its pages. Its
Christology starts and remains within just those 'generalities'
which liberation theologians deplore: though the concept of
the poor and the special place of the poor within the Gospel

is constantly invoked, for example, the precise nature and identity of the poor in Jesus' day remains unexamined. Those seeking a more concrete, contextual, Christology must look elsewhere.

The mysteries of Christ's infancy and hidden life (522–534)

The Catechism divides the mysteries of Christ's life into two groups, before and after the beginning of his public ministry. The first group opens with a section on the preparation for the coming of Christ – the 'rituals, sacrifices, figures and symbols' of the Old Covenant, the announcements of Israel's prophets, even the awakening in the hearts of pagans of 'a dim expectation of this coming'. It is not entirely clear what the authors have in mind in this reference to pagan expectation. Traditionally the passage in Virgil's Fourth Eclogue on the inauguration of a golden age by the birth of a marvellous child was understood as just such a prophecy. Maybe the authors are leaving a more general opening for a positive evaluation of the religious longing and expectations found in the ancient religions. At any rate, all this sense of expectation is summed up in the figure of John the Baptist, who embodies in his preaching, baptizing and martyrdom the witness of Israel to the coming deliverance of the Lord. The Church shares the pain and hope of humanity in search of salvation when she celebrates Advent each year. In doing so she enters liturgically into this ancient solidarity of expectant longing, and into the ministry and witness of John, who points beyond himself to him whom the Advent liturgy calls the 'desire of all nations', the Lamb of God who takes away the sins of the world (522–524).

The Catechism's brief treatment of the *Christmas mystery* concentrates on the paradox of the richness of the eternal God revealed in the poverty of a stable. Born into a poor family, revealed first to the poorest of men, the shepherds, the message of Christmas is of divine humility. And so to share in it we too must 'become a child', we must humble ourselves and become little. Christmas is thus the mystery of a 'marvellous exchange', in which Christ shares our poor humanity, so that we might enter into the riches of his divinity.

Following on from Christmas come Jesus' circumcision, his Epiphany or revelation to the Magi, his presentation in the temple, and the flight into Egypt (528–530). These are rather breathless paragraphs, which do little more than recapitulate the themes of the liturgy for these feast-days. It is worth noticing that, in a break with ancient tradition, the Catechism sees the circumcision of Jesus as a sign of his submission to the law of Israel, and as a prefiguration of baptism, but is silent on the more profound associations of this event with the Cross. In Catholic tradition, the circumcision was primarily seen as the first blood-shedding of Christ 'for us and for our salvation'. Western art is full of profound evocations of this first handing over of the child Jesus, from the nurturing arms of his mother to the world of men which will wound and ultimately kill him.

The paragraph on the slaughter of the innocents and the flight into Egypt is notable for the Catechism's only explicit description of Christ as 'the definitive liberator of God's people'. Though couched in rather general terms, its brief exploration of the theme of tyranny and persecution, and Christ's solidarity with those who still suffer in this way, has implications for any theology of liberation, and so an importance out of all proportion to the actual length of its treatment here (530).

By contrast with its brisk gallop through these great Christmas themes, the Catechism is much more expansive on the theme of Christ's hidden life at Nazareth, about which, of course, Scripture says virtually nothing. It is, however, a theme which has loomed large in modern Catholic teaching about the family, and Pope Paul VI delivered a famous speech on the family at Nazareth, which is read in the Liturgy of the Hours on the feast of the Holy Family, and quoted at length in this section. At first sight the theme here is that summed up in a verse now often omitted from renderings of the carol 'Once in Royal David's City':

Christian children all must be,
Mild, obedient, good as he.

But the Catechism moves beyond such moralism, and presents Jesus' obedience to Mary and Joseph not merely as a perfect fulfilment of the fourth commandment, but also as the mirror of the eternal Son's obedience to the Father, and of the obedience in suffering which would be his saving reversal of the disobedience of Adam. The extract from Pope Paul's Nazareth address extends even these great themes, not only to offer the home at Nazareth as the model for a family life rooted in simplicity and love, but also to see Christ, the carpenter's son, as sanctifying human work, holding up to all the world's workers 'their brother, who is God'.

There is a great deal to reflect on here, but catechists using this section with young people, especially those who have experienced the trauma of broken homes or abuse within the family, will certainly feel that this harmonious stress on love, simplicity and obedience has its limitations. The finding of Jesus in the temple is treated in this section as demonstrating the humble acceptance by Mary and Joseph of the mission of Jesus, despite their own imperfect understanding of it (534). The Lucan story, however, reveals a Christ capable of a startling single-mindedness which distressed and bewildered his parents, who had sought him for three days 'anxiously' or 'with sorrow'. The adolescent Christ, moreover, administers what can be read as a sharp rebuke to his mother, when she unwittingly places the claims of his earthly family before the will of the heavenly Father he has come to serve (Luke 2:41–51). There is a salty human and theological complexity in the scriptural story which is not done justice to by the Catechism's rather bland emphasis on obedience at this point.

The mysteries of Jesus' public life (535–560)

The Catechism's discussion of the public ministry of Jesus opens with a very fine discussion of his baptism by John. In this event, we are told, Christ accepts and begins his mission as the suffering servant of God, spoken of by Isaiah. He identifies himself with sinful humanity, thereby revealing himself as the Lamb who will take away the sin of the world, he anticipates the bloody baptism of his death. By his obedient acceptance of all this, as he tells John, he 'fulfils all righteousness', a phrase which however takes on resonances far beyond the baptism itself. The Father responds to this obedience with delighted and loving endorsement, and the Spirit rests on Christ as the waters of baptism are opened, a recapitulation of the Genesis narrative of creation: the baptism is thus a trinitarian event *par excellence*, and the prelude to the new creation which Christ's death and Resurrection would bring. Once again, the Catechism points to our sacramental and liturgical participation in this mystery. Through our own baptism we are assimilated to Christ in his baptism and death. We too enter this mystery of humble self-abasement and repentance, are reborn in the Spirit, and become the Father's beloved children in his Son: we too become a new creation (535–537).

The treatment of the temptations of Jesus in the wilderness after his baptism highlight some of the strengths and the weaknesses of the Catechism's handling of the gospels. As presented in Matthew's gospel, the temptations of Jesus are highly symbolic and stylized events, in which the figure of the new Adam and the new Israel recapitulates the temptations of Eden and of Israel's desert wanderings, but overcomes where they were defeated – as Newman's hymn has it:

O wisest love, that flesh and blood
Which did in Adam fail,
Should strive afresh against the foe,
Should strive and should prevail.

But these are no ordinary temptations, and Matthew does nothing to suggest that the Lord was internally troubled by them. Each of the devil's suggestions for a Messiahship based on power or miracle-mongering is rebuffed in a highly formalized way, with a quotation from the book of Deuteronomy. There is no attempt on the gospel-writer's part at psychological realism, and the whole incident has a symbolic and didactic feel to it, rather than that of an account of a real inner testing of Jesus' fidelity to the mission he has just inaugurated.

The Catechism's exposition of all this is excellent. It rightly draws out the way in which the story reverses the failures of Adam and Israel, it shows how Christ's victory over Satan here anticipates the victory on the Cross, and it points out that the temptations hold up a mirror to the true nature of Christ's Messiahship, which is one of humility and service, not of power and fascination. The victory of Christ is *'propter nos'*, for us and for our salvation: he binds the strong man on our behalf, and, once again, we enter into his victory liturgically and through the prayer-life of the Church, as we celebrate each year the forty days of Lent (539–540).

Yet this is not all that might have been said about the temptations of Jesus. There is a strand in the New Testament and in Catholic tradition which sees another dimension to all this. For the author of the epistle to the Hebrews the temptations of Jesus *were* real, internal temptations, felt along the nerves, and a cause of real struggle and anguish, so that 'because he himself has suffered and been tempted, he is able to help those who are tempted' (Hebrews 2:18). Jesus, it seems, suffered in his temptations, and to grasp their full meaning for us we need to penetrate beyond the apparently effortless text-swapping put-down of the devil in Matthew's account.

There are theological problems here. Much of the force of temptation in our cases comes from our innate sinfulness – our cultivated blindness to the spiritual reality of the choices we are faced with, our callousness towards others, our selfish instincts enormously strengthened by habitual surrender. Our temptations come from within our psyche, where sin is lodged and naturalized. But how must it be for one who is sinless, who has never allowed a thick scab of indifference to form over the wound of love and openness to others? How must it be for someone whose will is lovingly conformed to the will of the Father, whose eyes are open to the reality of the spiritual struggle going on all around them? Surely for such a person temptation must be external, not internalized, and so, different in kind, and easier to resist? By and large, that is the view that has predominated in the Catholic tradition, but its limitations are obvious. However we express it, any such view must in the end tend to distance Christ, by weakening the claim of the epistle to the Hebrews that we really do have a great high priest 'able to sympathize with our weakness', one who 'in every respect has been tempted as we are, but without sin' (Hebrews 4:14–16). In our own time, perhaps the profoundest theological exploration of the suffering of Jesus has been the work of the Swiss priest Hans Urs von Balthasar. For von Balthasar, this aspect of traditional Catholic thinking about the temptations of Jesus fails to express the depth of the love and vulnerability, the solidarity in suffering, which the Incarnation entailed. The temptations of Jesus, he argues, were real agony, undergone when Jesus was weak from fasting, felt in the heart and mind of God incarnate. Jesus, according to von Balthasar, was plunged 'up to the throat' in the waters of temptation. So in the Matthean story Jesus' use of Deuteronomy to drive back the tempter is not the tranquil vanquishing of a weaker opponent. Though not concerned with the 'banal issues' that make up our trials, the temptations of the Messiah are nevertheless exactly like our struggles in faith to discern and do the will of God – 'he knows what it means to be held back from the abyss by the single thread of a word from God'. For, says von Balthasar, 'he must be able to taste the full attack of demonic temptation in order to know its true power and plausibility'. Jesus himself must be able to apply to himself Paul's words, 'When I am weak, then I am strong', and God himself 'does the unthinkable: he exposes himself to Satan's fascination, in order to burst the dazzling bubble *from within*'.[9]

The religious power and value of this interpretation of the temptations is obvious, but it is not one that the Catechism's resolutely 'from above' Christology can easily accommodate. As we shall see, even the implications of the agony in Gethsemane for Christ's interior suffering are passed over in the

Catechism in a single sentence (612), and the opportunity to explore a dimension of Christology which has great consolatory and evangelical value is not taken. This is all the more striking given that the influence of von Balthasar on other aspects of the Catechism is very marked.

The Kingdom of God (541–560)

The rest of the Catechism's treatment of the public ministry of Jesus, up to his entry into Jerusalem, is arranged around the general theme of the Kingdom of God. Proclamation of the coming of the Kingdom was clearly fundamental to Jesus' own preaching, and the whole notion of Messiahship, the foretold Anointed King, is intimately linked to it. Jesus inaugurates the Kingdom by his preaching, and the Father calls men and women to gather round his Son in response to his preaching. This gathering is the Church, 'on earth the seed and beginning of that kingdom'. All are called to enter the Kingdom, but it belongs especially to the poor and the humble, to children, to the 'little ones' of the earth, and to sinners. Jesus himself 'shares the life of the poor, from the cradle to the cross: he experiences hunger, thirst and privation', and so 'identifies himself with the poor of every kind, and makes active love towards them the condition for entry to his kingdom' (544, 559). The parables of Jesus are a call to a radical choice, to give up everything else in order to gain the Kingdom, and his miracles are messianic signs, challenging belief in him but also a cause of offence. In his miracles Jesus overthrows the kingdom of Satan, and gives a foretaste of the liberation of men and women from all that oppresses them – hunger, illness, injustice, death. But the Kingdom, which 'will be definitively established through Christ's Cross', is not yet fulfilled, and he did not come to abolish all evils here below: his principal target is sin, which is the root of all human bondage (546–550).

In this Kingdom, the twelve apostles have a special place, destined to sit on thrones of judgement, and to carry on Christ's work of proclaiming the Kingdom. The Catechism, however, takes the opportunity of the apostolic theme to develop what seems at this point an over-enthusiastic emphasis on the role of Peter. The 'kingdom' theme modulates into a discussion of the 'keys of the kingdom', and to the power of the apostles to bind and loose, understood as Christ's commission 'to absolve sins, to pronounce doctrinal judgements, and to make disciplinary decisions in the Church'. In particular, this ministry is entrusted to Peter, 'the only one to whom [Christ] specifically entrusted the keys of the kingdom' (551–553). This passage takes up a fifth of the whole space given to the kingdom theme, and seems both disproportionate and inappropriate at this point in the Catechism, given the lengthy consideration of these matters later, under the article on the holy catholic Church. Moreover, the reading offered here of the granting of the keys to Peter is certainly unnecessarily exclusive. The commission to declare the forgiveness of sins, to teach and to take decisions for the common good and right ordering of the people of God, belongs to the whole Church, and to all its pastors, not to a single apostle or bishop. To place this emphasis on power and authority at this point in the Catechism, before any proper discussion of the nature of the Church in itself, is certainly to reverse the priorities so carefully embodied in the structure of *Lumen Gentium*, and thereby to depart from one of the fundamental emphases of the Council.

Helpful though this section on the Kingdom is in general, there is a tendency to see the Kingdom as something already achieved – 'definitively established through Christ's Cross', and begun in the Church. Yet we pray each day 'thy kingdom come', and there is perhaps too little sense in this part of the Catechism of the element of as yet unfulfilled hope in our belief in the Kingdom. It follows *Lumen Gentium* in calling the Church the 'seed and beginning of the kingdom', but the Council's text goes on, as the Catechism does not, to emphasize that the Kingdom is as yet incomplete, and that the Church is still a traveller on the way towards her fulfilment – 'While she slowly grows to maturity, the Church longs for the completed kingdom, and with all her strength, hopes and desires to be united in glory with her king.'[10]

The discussion of the Kingdom culminates in an account of the Transfiguration of Christ, and then of his entry as Messiah into the holy city of Jerusalem. The Transfiguration, like the Baptism, brings out the best in the Catechism, in a rich discussion of the interweaving themes embedded in the gospel story. Like the Baptism the Transfiguration is a trinitarian event, in which the voice of the Father witnesses to the mission and authority of the Son, and the cloud indicates his overshadowing by the Holy Spirit. This, as in the overshadowing of the tent in the book of Exodus, is the place of meeting between heaven and earth. Moses and Elijah represent the witness of law and prophets to the Messiah, and Christ's glory is, in St Thomas' words, 'the sacrament of the second regeneration', that is, a foreshadowing of the mystery of our own resurrection. This resurrection is shared now in the sacraments of the Church but they, like the Transfiguration itself, offer us a share not simply in glory, but in the sufferings of the Messiah who comes not to an earthly throne, but to the glory of the Cross. This paradox is clinched in a magnificent quotation from St Augustine, which catches the light and the shadow of the scene as Christ and the disciples descend from the mountain of Transfiguration, and Christ reveals to them the unwelcome truth that the Messiah, and his disciples, will triumph not in earthly glory, but in the way of the Cross:

> Life goes down to be killed; Bread goes down to suffer hunger; the Way goes down to be exhausted on his journey; the Spring goes down to suffer thirst; and you refuse to suffer? (556)

Luke tells us that Moses and Elijah spoke with Jesus of the 'Exodus' he was to accomplish in Jerusalem. The Holy City is the place where he becomes the Passover Lamb. The city of David is the place where the Son of David will die. The Messiah enters his city to cries of acclamation, but not, however, as an earthly king. He comes in a humility which prefigures the humility that belongs to the Church, and his subjects are children and the poor. We identify ourselves with these, the lowly ones, the '*pueri Hebraeorum*', when we commemorate the Lord's Passover in the Holy Week liturgy, starting with the Palm Sunday celebration of Christ's entry into Jerusalem. We enact it, too, every Sunday when, with the singing of the Sanctus, we begin the memorial of the Passover of the Lord (559–560). And so the Messianic theme, the Kingdom of God, and the Church's defining celebration of her identity in the Eucharist, is rooted in an identification with the poor and the lowly.

JESUS CHRIST SUFFERED UNDER PONTIUS PILATE, WAS CRUCIFIED, DIED, AND WAS BURIED

Jesus and Israel

To talk of the Messiah, to name Jesus Christ, is to locate the saving work of God firmly within the history of a single people. Jesus was a Jew, a truth which has been brought home by a flood of modern research, and which has probably been the single most significant contribution of modern biblical studies to our understanding of the Gospels.[11] Yet this research, valuable as it is, was not needed for the Church to know of its indebtedness to the people of the Old Covenant. Christ is the expectation of Israel, and all the categories which we use to speak of his work – the Lamb of God, the redeemer, the sacrifice for our sins – are borrowed from Israel's faith, the faith that shaped him, and without which he cannot be understood The Scriptures he revered and in which he found the key to his own mission were Israel's Scriptures, and remain definitive for us. Salvation is of the Jews.

Yet this is an admission which has stuck in the throats of Christians, generation after generation. Already within the New Testament we see evidence of the growing conflict between the members of the infant Church and the synagogues which nurtured and, in the Roman world, sheltered and protected them. New Testament scholarship sees in

much of the conflict between Jesus and his Jewish contemporaries, especially the Pharisees, a dramatization of the
experience of the Church, 'cast out of the synagogues'. St
John's gospel is shot through with a profound ambivalence to
the Jewish people, especially the Jewish religious leaders, and
their apparent blindness to the light which had shone among
them.

In such considerations lie the origins of the long and
shameful history of Christian anti-Semitism. Israel had, it
seemed, rejected the Messiah, and the Church now, not the
synagogue, was the true Israel of God. But Israel's sin, it came
to be thought, was more than the mere rejection of the
Messiah. Building on texts like Matthew 27:25, 'His blood be
on us, and on our children', Christians came to lay the
principal blame for the death of the Son of God at the door
of the Jews. Till the 1960s, the Church read in her liturgy each
Good Friday a devastating sermon by St Augustine on Psalm
63:

> Let not the Jews say, 'we did not kill Christ'. For they delivered
> him up to Pilate, the judge, that they might seem innocent of
> his death ... What Pilate did made him a partaker in their
> crime. But in comparison with them, he was much more
> innocent ...[12]

In the Middle Ages a vicious anti-Jewish tradition grew up
among Christians, and bred legends that Jews sought to
recrucify Christ by stealing and stabbing the Host, or by
ritually murdering Christian children, in a gruesome parody
of the Cross. To this day, the curious tourist can see some of
these legends depicted in the Blessed Sacrament chapel in
Orvieto cathedral. All over Europe innocent Jews were tor-
tured and killed in pursuit of this murderous fantasy, and it
was revived by anti-Semitic agitators and writers in Europe in
the early twentieth century, and helped to nourish Nazism.

The Church bears a heavy responsibility for much of this,
and it was slow to make amends: it was not till the time of
Pope John XXIII that the offensive reference to the 'perfi-
dious Jews' was dropped from the solemn intercessions in the

liturgy of Good Friday. The Second Vatican Council, however, turned its back decisively on all theological justification of anti-Semitism in its declaration on the Jews in *Nostra Aetate.* This document at last solemnly acknowledged the Church's indebtedness to the Jewish people for the handing on of the revelation of God, affirmed God's continuing love for his chosen people, and denied that Israel had been cast off or cursed by God. It explicitly stated that despite the role of the Jewish authorities in the death of Christ, neither all Jews then, nor the Jewish people today, could be blamed for his Passion. Christ died because of the sins of the whole human race.[13]

It is against this background, as well as that of modern research on the Jewish context of Jesus' message, that we need to understand the lengthy discussion of the relationship of Jesus to the people and religion of Israel which opens its discussion of his death on the Cross. Jesus was indeed 'rejected by the elders and chief priests and the scribes', but he was also handed over to the Gentiles: his death was at the hands of the Romans (572). How then are we to understand the role of Israel in the death of the Messiah?

The Catechism is clear that many Jews believed in Jesus – members of the Sanhedrin like Joseph of Arimathea, Pharisees like Nicodemus. The Acts of the Apostles tell us of the many priests and the thousands of Jews, including some of the Pharisees, who believed after Pentecost (595). Jesus had much in common with the Pharisees, not least a shared belief in the resurrection of the dead and many pious practices and attitudes, and he often mixed and dined with them. Nevertheless, there was much in his teaching which alienated his Jewish contemporaries, and persuaded them that he was acting 'against the essential institutions of the Chosen People' (576). The Catechism identifies three such issues – Jesus' attitude to the law, his relation to the temple, and his apparently blasphemous identification of himself with the one God, whose glory, Israel believed, no human being can share.

Christians have conventionally opposed law to Gospel, and have seen the Old Testament law as a crushing burden, the dead letter that oppresses by making impossible demands. Yet this thinking is in striking contrast with the joy and delight in the law so often celebrated in the Old Testament, for example in Psalm 19:

> The law of the Lord is perfect, reviving the soul;
> the testimony of the Lord is sure, making wise the simple;
> the precepts of the Lord are right, rejoicing the heart;
> the commandment of the Lord is pure, enlightening the
>   eyes . . .
> more to be desired are they than gold, even much fine gold;
> sweeter also than honey, and drippings of the honey-comb.

Clearly, 'law' in such a context is a hopelessly inadequate translation of the Hebrew word 'Torah'. 'Torah' for ancient Israel was far more than law – it was a God-given revelation of the roots of reality, and to conform to it meant not slavish obedience to petty rules, but a joyous co-operation with the revealed will of God. In Christian belief, of course, only one human being could do this, for only one will and one heart was perfectly in tune with the will and the heart of God – Jesus alone can fulfil the Torah (578). But he taught to all who listened to him this rich and life-giving understanding of the law as the liberating revelation of the love of God, and he taught this 'as one who had authority, and not as their scribes' (581). This *authority* of Jesus does not mean that his teaching had some sort of official backing, it means, quite literally that he was its *author*, that it came from within, and not at second hand. For Jesus, like the psalmist, and like the prophet Jeremiah, the law was written in the heart, above all in the heart of the Suffering Servant, who by his suffering obedience redeems all who have transgressed the Covenant (580). Thus, although Jesus' teaching on the law brought down on him the anger of those who understood it in a narrower and more restrictive sense, his teaching was not a repudiation of the law, but was itself derived from the understanding of the Torah in the prophetic tradition of Israel.

   In the same way, the Catechism argues that Jesus did not set himself in opposition to the temple, but reverenced it and understood himself in the light of the temple tradition. He regularly came up to Jerusalem to worship at the temple at the great feasts, he paid the temple tax, he drove the sellers out from its courts. After his Resurrection, his disciples worshipped daily in the temple. He did predict its downfall, but as part of his expectation of the last days, which his own Passion would inaugurate, and he used the metaphor of the temple as God's dwelling-place as a way of expressing his own role and nature as the dwelling-place of God among men (586).[14]

The Catechism sees the 'true stumbling block' for Jesus' Jewish opponents in the role he claimed in the forgiveness of sins. Christ ate with sinners as freely and familiarly as with the righteous Pharisees. His table-fellowship with sinners, however, went beyond simple generosity. Jesus identified his own merciful conduct towards the sinful with the mercy of God. His claim to forgive sins – endorsed by his ability to heal – constituted a religious claim which Israel's leaders could neither accept nor tolerate, for 'who can forgive sins but God alone?' The Catechism sees in this claim to forgive sins an explicit claim to divinity, equivalent to the Johannine 'I am' sayings (590). In the end, the failure of what the Catechism calls 'certain Jews' to accept Jesus' claim to forgive sins is a failure to recognize God made man (594). This may be to project a developed understanding of the Church's faith inappropriately into the lifetime of Jesus, but there is little doubt that Jesus' claim to speak for God in welcoming sinners to forgiveness and admitting them among his followers did indeed constitute the heart of his 'scandal' for the men and women of his time, just as it constituted the heart of the work of salvation he came to achieve.

Appropriately, therefore, the Catechism's discussion of the reasons for Christ's condemnation concludes with an insistence that it was sin that brought Jesus to the Cross, and the sinful human race as a whole, not the Jewish people, bear responsibility for his death. There is a redeeming irony in the fact that the Good Friday liturgy, in which as we have seen so much anti-Semitism once found a lodging, should also have preserved at its very heart an ancient and moving ceremony which embodies this profound truth of our universal responsibility for the death of Christ. As the people come to kiss the foot of the Cross, the choir sing the Reproaches, sentences of rebuke and lamentation adapted from the Scriptures, apparently addressed to the people of Israel, but here of course redirected, and spoken to all who come to kneel at the feet of the one who bears their sins:

> My people, what have I done to you?
> How have I offended you? Answer me.
> I led you from slavery to freedom,
> and drowned your captors in the sea,
> but you handed me over to your high priests.
> I gave you saving water from the rock,
> but you gave me vinegar and gall to drink.
> I gave you a royal sceptre,
> but you gave me a crown of thorns.

CHRIST'S REDEMPTIVE DEATH IN GOD'S PLAN OF SALVATION

Why did Jesus Christ die on the Cross? Was the crucifixion a piece of bad luck, or was it fundamental in the plan of God for salvation? Might Jesus have redeemed us without shedding his blood? What was it about this death, and the manner of it, which made it the focal point and pivot of human healing and human salvation?

There are no questions deeper than these in the whole of Christian theology, and no questions in Christian theology have led so often and so disastrously to mistaken and sub-Christian conceptions of God. Christian men and women have imagined that on Calvary Christ appeased the anger of an outraged and offended God, defusing the wrath which would otherwise consume us. They have thought of God as appeasable only by blood, by a death, if not the death of the guilty, then the death of the innocent in their place. They have imagined that Calvary shows us the anger of God the Father at odds with the mercy of God the Son.

The whole matter is made more difficult by the difficulty of discovering what Jesus himself taught concerning his death. The Catechism sees in the Lord's statement in Mark's gospel that 'the Son of Man came ... to give his life as a ransom for many' a deliberate reference to what is said of the Suffering Servant in Isaiah 53, 'he makes himself an offering for sin'. Many commentators think, however, that this saying reflects mature Christian reflection on the meaning of the Lord's death, rather than the Lord's own words in his lifetime. But if that is so, it seems likely that the Marcan saying is shaped by the words spoken by Christ at the Last Supper, 'this is my body, given for you', and it is in fact this eucharistic dimension of the death of Jesus, rooted in Christ's own description of his death as an offering for others, which shapes all that the Catechism has to say on the subject. We will not find here any very revolutionary interpretation of the meaning of the death of Jesus for our times: as other commentators have pointed out, this section could have been written at almost any point in the last few centuries, and it is perhaps disappointing that the Catechism has not searched for ways of renewing our sense of the meaning of this mysterious death which is the centre of our faith. Yet if it is unoriginal, the Catechism's account of the meaning of the death of Jesus escapes the sub-Christian diminishments of the love and mercy of God which so often disfigure talk about the atonement, and it offers a profoundly scriptural and trinitarian account of the meaning of the Cross.

For the Catechism, the death of Jesus is, from beginning to end, an offering. It is, in the first place, an offering not *to* but *from* God the Father, who surrenders his beloved Son into the hands of men, making him to be sin 'who knew no sin, so that in him we might become the righteousness of God'. The process of abandonment of Jesus, 'handed over' by the traitor Judas, handed over by his own people to the Romans, and handed over by Pilate to be crucified, is a letting go by God, a parting from his Son and Word, so that the Son might stand in solidarity with the abandoned state of humanity, lost in sin (602–603). The cry of desolation on the Cross, 'My God, my God, why have you forsaken me?', is the measure not only of the suffering of the Son, but of the costly giving of the Father.

The Cross is also the offering of the Son, who surrenders himself in loving obedience to the will of the Father, so that the world might live. His meat and drink is to do the will of the one who sends him, and he accepts the cup of suffering which the Father places before him. It is for that bitter cup, out of which will flow water for the healing of the nations, that he cries out on the Cross, 'I thirst' (606–607). That self-offering is accomplished and expressed at the Last Supper, and it is by sharing the cup of the Eucharist that we too can share in the self-offering of the Son to the Father. That eucharistic involvement is incarnated in our Christian lives, as we share the cup of the Lord's sufferings by imitating him, following him on the way of suffering (618).

The New Testament has many different ways of describing the effect of the death of Jesus – justification, salvation, reconciliation, expiation, redemption, freedom, sanctifica-tion, new creation. The Catechism too uses a wide range of metaphors to expound the meaning of the Cross. But all these concepts are brought into focus in the central theme of the loving obedience and offering of the Son to the Father. So when the Catechism speaks of the death of Christ as a 'substitution', a concept with associations of God's wrath being taken out on an innocent victim in place of the guilty, it sees this substitution as one of obedience for disobedience. Substitution thus becomes part of the wider concept of recapitulation, as Christ in suffering undoes the mistakes of erring humanity (615).

In all this the controlling idea is that the Cross in some mysterious way is not imposed from without, a mere fact of the history of sin in this world, but that it represents, indeed is the sacrament, of the life of love within God himself. The crucified humanity of Jesus is the 'free and perfect instrument' of the divine love (609), and the Cross is what the love of Father, Son and Spirit *looks like* when it is lived out in this world. Within the Godhead self-giving love, with no barriers and no defences, bubbles over in joy, in unlimited life, sharing, and mutual delight – love is pure community. But in our fallen world, to live such a life of love means the opposite – it brings grief and oppression, disaster, confrontation, the lonely death of the Cross. To be totally vulnerable, totally open to others and without barriers in our world, as Christ was, is to become pure victim. The Dominican theologian Herbert McCabe has suggested that we can get a grip on this if we imagine the life of the Trinity as a picture projected on to a screen: where the screen is smooth, flat and silvered, the image will be true and undistorted. But now imagine the image projected not on to a screen, but on to a rubbish tip – it would be totally transformed, unrecognizable. The Cross is what the love of the Trinity looks like projected on to the rubbish tip our sin has made of the world.[15]

Such an understanding calls us to re-examine all our categories, for in this perspective nothing will be what it seems to our unregenerate eyes: the Cross challenges all our values. The powerlessness of Christ on the Cross, for example, is not the absence or withdrawal of God's power, it is what the power of God is like in our world. God's power looks like weakness because it has nothing in common with what we think of as power, the force behind the mailed fist or the jackboot, the triumph of the strong over the weak. Thus the Cross is not simply the way in which God comes to help the world, it is God's self-disclosure 'in what is most deeply his own'.[16] And so in the Eucharist, as in the death of Jesus, these paradoxes are gathered up, as the slaughtered victim of human fear and hatred becomes the root of love and reconciliation in a community where no-one wields power as the world knows it, where everything is self-gift, God's gift to us, and, in Christ, ours to God.

There is, therefore, great richness in what the Catechism has to say about the death of Jesus. Yet its reluctance to speak of the limitations of the Incarnation once again blurs the full impact of its overall message. In its single paragraph on the cost of this to Christ, as represented in Gethsemane (612), the Catechism is concerned primarily to emphasize his acceptance of the will of the Father. The horror and suffering this involved is evoked in a single line on Christ's prayer that this cup might pass. 'Thus he expresses the horror that death represented for his human nature.' But more should surely have been said here. The Catechism is anxious to emphasize the transcendent dignity of the person of Jesus Christ, yet its reticence here is misplaced, for that very dignity must surely have had implications for the suffering of Jesus. For us, distance from God has lost some of its true horror, because it is our daily condition. Sin, at one level, is for us a sort of contentment, a willingness to live in the half-light, away from God. Only one like Jesus, who lived to and for God, who knew himself only as derived from and obedient to his Father, could feel the full horror of the alienation of sin which descended upon him in the Passion. Only he could feel what it was to be human, yet cast out of God's presence, only he knew the cost of sin. Paradoxically, his very closeness to God makes the experience of distance intolerable, and his human frailty becomes the mirror or icon of his unique dignity as the only Son of God. His prayer in Gethsemane embodies this paradox, for he begins it with the invocation 'Abba', that uniquely intimate address to his loving Father. He goes on, however, 'not my will, but thine be done'. This is the only place in the gospels where it is even suggested that Christ's will and that of his Father, so intimately in tune, might diverge. It should give us pause, for it throws a devastating shaft of light on the desolation that was coming upon Jesus, a desolation which would culminate in the great cry of abandonment on the Cross, as he calls out to a God whose presence he no longer felt, not now using the term Abba, but the impersonal 'My God, my God, why have you forsaken me?'

BURIAL AND DESCENT INTO HELL

Had the Catechism been composed even a few years ago it might well have passed quickly over the burial of Jesus and his descent into hell with little comment. Instead it devotes nine paragraphs to these associated mysteries, in an extended reflection on the dead Christ. Symbolically, Holy Saturday is the sabbath rest of God after the new creation, the work of which Christ on the Cross declared 'It is accomplished'. So now, as in the beginning, God 'rested from all his work which he had done in Creation' (Genesis 2:3; 624). The Catechism presses beyond this interpretation of the work of the Cross as the refashioning of a world deformed by sin. The eternal Word of God remains united to the dead humanity of Christ, body and soul. As St Thomas says, on Holy Saturday God is not only a man, but a dead man.[17] God himself is dead, and has joined humanity in its worst extreme. The 'hell' spoken of in this article of the Creed is the 'sheol' of the Bible, the place of dim unreal afterlife in which there is no vision of God and hence no real human fulfilment. It is 'limbo', the state in which, as the Church speculates, the souls of the just were confined before the Passion and Resurrection. But it means more than this. Von Balthasar says somewhere that in the Incarnation God comes to humankind in its worst extremity, 'at its wits' end'. Here, in the tomb and in the descent into hell which the tomb symbolizes, all human hope ends, and there is nothing but desolation. Yet even here Christ walks in solidarity with us, God spares himself nothing. In Christian tradition the descent of Christ among the dead has generally been understood as a descent in triumph: Christ comes to shatter the doors of death and to rescue all the just who have died in hope, from Adam to John the Baptist. The 'Harrowing of Hell' was a constant theme in medieval art and drama, with Christ striding over the fallen gates of hell, under which the devil lies squashed. But there is another and complementary way of understanding this triumph of Christ. He does indeed enter hell to take possession of it, as St Thomas says, but that 'taking possession' is like his taking possession of human nature, it is a costly act of solidarity, the last act of the emptying of the Incarnation. The great theologian of this understanding of the descent into hell is Hans Urs von Balthasar, and he has dared to suggest that in this great mystery we are given grounds to hope that even in hell, even for the damned, the redemption of God is inexhaustible. Traditional thinking about the Harrowing of Hell has Christ descend to hell to rescue the just. Von Balthasar sees in Christ's identification with the dead in hell as achieving even more, and as holding out hope that in his infinite mercy God will frustrate even the will of the damned to isolate themselves from him, that he will let none of his children fall away from him and be lost. Here, says von Balthasar,

> lies hope for the person who refusing all love, damns himself. This man who wants to be totally alone, will he not after all find beside him in Sheol Someone still lonelier, the Son forsaken by the Father, who will prevent him from experiencing his self-chosen Hell to the end.[18]

Whether we go as far along this line of thought as von Balthasar or not, his general approach seems to underlie this whole section of the Catechism, and to shape its teaching that

> The descent into hell brings the Gospel message of salvation to complete fulfilment. This is the last phase of Jesus' messianic mission, a phase condensed in time but vast in significance: the spread of Christ's redemptive work to all men of all times and all places ... (634)

THE RESURRECTION AND ASCENSION

The Catechism recognizes in the Resurrection 'the crowning truth of our faith in Christ', but its treatment of it is in fact surprisingly brief. It has three basic points to make. The Resurrection is a real historical event, established by the fact of the empty tomb, and not merely a new understanding of Christ's significance by the disciples at Easter. To make this point, the Catechism emphasizes the demoralization of the disciples on Good Friday, and the shock and reluctance to believe which marks all the resurrection narratives. So, 'the hypothesis that the Resurrection was produced by the apostles' faith (or credulity) will not hold up. On the contrary, their faith in the Resurrection was born, under the action of divine grace, from their direct experience of the risen Jesus' (638–644).

Yet, despite this, the Resurrection is also an event which transcends historical categories. No-one witnessed or could witness what 'happened' on Easter morning. It is not an event perceptible to the senses (647), and it is in no sense a 'return' by Christ to earthly life (as the resurrection of Jairus' daughter or of Lazarus were). The risen Christ passes 'to another life beyond time and space' (645–646). The Resurrection is thus a 'mystery of faith', intelligible only to those who, by the power of the Holy Spirit, believe the apostolic testimony. This teaching is very compressed, but crucial for our understanding of what is meant when we speak, as we must, of the historicity of the Resurrection. The Catechism wants to hold together, as the New Testament itself does, both the claim that the Resurrection is something real, something which truly happened, and not merely a psychological 'lift' for the disciples, and yet the truth that it is not an event in the same sense as the crucifixion is an event. Rather, it is God's decisive revelation of what the event of the Cross *means*, a laying bare of the divine reality which underlies the human catastrophe of the crucifixion. The Catechism seems to be following an essentially Johannine understanding of the Cross and Resurrection here, for in John's gospel Christ's 'hour', in which his glory is revealed, is not the Resurrection, but his 'lifting up' on the Cross. For John, one might even say, the Resurrection and the Ascension happen simultaneously with the crucifixion, and Easter morning is in reality the unfolding of what is already achieved on Good Friday.

The third point made in this section of the Catechism is that the Resurrection is a trinitarian event. The Father raises up the Son, the Son is vindicated and established as Lord of creation, and the Spirit which fills him and is the instrument of resurrection is given to us, to cleanse us from sin and to create in us a new life, making us children of God in our turn and brethren of the risen Christ. The Resurrection, like the Incarnation, is *'propter nos'*, for us and for our salvation: it is the principle and source of *our* future resurrection. Because of it, Christ by his Spirit lives in our hearts, a life orientated towards God and the age to come (654–655). This new life will be the subject of the final section of the Catechism's treatment of the Creed.

If the Resurrection is the revelation of the inner meaning of the crucifixion, the Ascension is in some sense a comment on the meaning of the Resurrection. The Catechism's handling of Scripture at this point, it has to be said, is neither very satisfactory nor entirely consistent, notably in its use of material from St John's gospel. The story of Christ's appearance to Mary Magdalene on Easter morning is used to establish that the Ascension is an 'historical and transcendent event'. This is very unsatisfactory, because for St John the Ascension appears not to have been a distinct event at all, but a gradually revealed dimension of the Resurrection itself. There is no narrative in John of a symbolic departure into the clouds, in stark contrast to the developing story found in Luke and Acts. Instead, in John's version Christ on Easter morning forbids Mary to touch him, because he has 'not yet ascended' to the Father: but that same evening he breathes the Spirit on the apostles, the Pentecostal gift which in the Acts of the Apostles flows from his Ascension. The event which Luke places at the end of forty days appears in John's gospel to have happened invisibly in the course of the first Easter day, and in John's gospel there is no decisive 'final encounter' of the disciples with Jesus, before his 'irreversible entry' into glory, of the sort the Catechism discusses (659). In fact what is important for the New Testament is not the 'event', but the significance of Christ's return into the bosom of the Father, and his enthronement as Lord of all. In Luther's words, there is a man in heaven. Our human nature, alienated from God by sin, is now inseparably joined to the Godhead in glory, no longer in the humiliation of a suffering mortal man, but in the triumphant glory which is our assurance that one day all shall be well, and all manner of things shall be well. In the heart of God, a human being stands and prays for the whole of humanity. A man sits on the throne of God. Nothing can separate us from the love of God which is in Christ. So the Ascension is not about the absence of Christ from the world, his departure, leaving us gazing after him. In ascending he is made Lord of all, and this means that he is enthroned in the heart of reality, for the throne of God is in the heart of creation. His dominion is not in another world, but in this one, over 'all peoples, nations, and languages', and the Church lives to image forth his rule, proclaiming here and now his peace, forgiveness and reconciling presence, through his Spirit.

He will come again in glory, to judge the living and the dead

That presence and rule exists in the Church, however, only incompletely, 'in mystery'. We live now in a provisional age, and the Church itself is marked with the mortality of things that will pass away, groaning in travail as we wait the revelation of the Sons of God (671). The Eucharist is at one and the same time the sacrament of his presence amongst us, and the great sacrament of expectation, speaking of the brokenness of this world and pointing us to the healing we long for beyond this world, as we pray for Christ's return, 'Maranatha, Our Lord come'. We live, says the Catechism in 'a time of waiting and watching'.

What does this strange language mean? What are we waiting for? The Scripture language, and the language of the Catechism following Scripture, is picture-language. Readers of this section of the Catechism are likely to find it baffling, with its talk of final tribulations, of the conversion of Israel which must precede the end, and with its discussion of the mysterious figure of Antichrist. There is a temptation to pass quickly over all this, impatiently or in puzzlement. In fact, issues of absolutely fundamental importance are being discussed here. They do, however, need some deciphering.

We naturally think and talk of Christ's return as an 'event', the last event of all which will bring the world to an end, and we picture it, as Jesus himself and the writers of the New Testament did, as a great court of justice, with books, a judgement seat, and so on. The Catechism is careful not to dwell on such imagery, however, for it wants to point us beyond the images to the inner meaning. Just as creation is precisely not the first in a series of events in time, but the declaration that time and event themselves have a meaning, so our faith in the return of Christ in judgement is not a belief in one more event, one more thing that happens. Instead, it is the belief that in the end God will make all events add up, that our broken world will be mended, that the longings of our hearts for justice and truth will be satisfied. *How* that can be we cannot know, any more than we can know how a dead man can be raised to a glorious but to us invisible life. But the Catechism, while affirming the place of this truth in the Creed, is concerned to make us understand that the value of this teaching is primarily negative, that we are given this belief as a kind of disinfectant. It is designed not so much to provide a detailed scenario of the last days, for it is beyond imagining, as to free us from idolatry and the false expectation that these, our deepest longings, can ever be satisfied in *this* world. Our world is the world which crucified the Lord of glory, which had its chance of welcoming him who was perfect truth, perfect justice, and which instead nailed him to a tree. The doctrine of original sin tells us that from the dawn of time our world was askew, at odds with its creator: the doctrine of the final judgement tells us that the world will go on like that, that Christ will be crucified till the end of time, as mankind goes on oppressing the poor, enthroning lies, denying God, to the very end. To believe in the judgement of Christ is therefore to know the weight of human sinfulness, to be aware that no earthly state will ever really meet the needs of its citizens, that no human system will ever be truly just. But more than that, it is also to confess Jesus and no-one else as Lord. It is to refuse to settle for anything less than perfect righteousness, to refuse to lower our sights and be *satisfied* with what this world offers, and to affirm that in the end God's righteousness will be vindicated, his Christ will reign. This could be and sometimes has been a recipe for passive other-worldliness, which leaves the tyrants to get on with crushing the weak, or refuses to struggle for justice for the oppressed, since we know that sin will always frustrate such attempts. But it need not and should not be so. The apocalyptic language of judgement, so strange to our modern ears, has again and again served Israel and then the Church as a radical criticism of tyranny. Our faith in the coming rule of Christ gives us a glimpse of what perfect love and justice are, a measure by which to assess worldly claims to justice and right, a pattern to reach out towards, and a hope to live by, even though we know that in this order of things we can never fully realize it.

So we need to be aware of the way in which the Catechism points us beyond the picture language to this radical understanding of God's judgement. For the Catechism Antichrist is not merely some mysterious figure in the last days, it is the false claim of any system which tries to deceive people into accepting an earthly kingdom in place of the Kingdom of God, what the Catechism calls 'secular messianism'. The authors probably had Marxism in mind here, but what they say reaches far beyond any particular target, and calls us to a vigilance which is a fundamental part of faith in the risen Lord.

The Catechism's last word on judgement in this section takes up once again an emphasis from St John's gospel. The judgement of the last day is happening now, every day, as we respond or fail to respond to God's grace. 'This is the judgement', says St John, 'that the light has come into the world, and men loved darkness rather than light, because their deeds were evil' (John 3:19). When Christ stood crowned with thorns and in a mock royal robe before Pilate, judgement was being passed not on Jesus but on the sceptres, crowns, empires and dynasties, the 'powers of this age' which were crucifying the Lord of glory. That same judgement is enacted in every age, and every time we turn away from God's self-giving to us in grace and in the need of our brothers and sisters. The deepest truth about the judgement of Christ is that he does not judge at all: 'For God sent the Son into the world, not to condemn the world, but that the world might be saved through him.' As the Catechism explains, 'By rejecting grace in this life, one already judges oneself . . .' (679). This profound Johannine truth is captured in Charles Causley's version of an inscription from a French seventeenth-century crucifix:

I am the great sun, but you do not see me,
I am your husband, but you turn away.
I am the captive, but you do not free me,
I am the captain you will not obey.

I am the truth, but you will not believe me,
I am the city where you will not stay,
I am your wife, your child, but you will leave me,
I am that God to whom you will not pray,

I am your counsel, but you do not hear me,
I am the lover you will betray,
I am the victor, but you do not cheer me,
I am the holy dove whom you will slay.

I am your life, but if you will not name me,
Seal up your soul with tears, and never blame me.[19]

NOTES

1 F. von Hügel, *The Mystical Element of Religion* (London, 1923), vol. I, pp. 26–7.
2 This is profoundly explored in Hans Urs von Balthasar, *Mysterium Paschale* (Edinburgh, 1990), chapter 1.
3 *Collected Poems of Stevie Smith* (Harmondsworth, 1985), pp. 389–90.
4 Quoted in A. Nichols, *The Theology of Joseph Ratzinger* (Edinburgh, 1988), p. 113.
5 On medieval devotion to the Holy Name of Jesus see my *The Stripping of the Altars* (London and New Haven, 1992), pp. 236–8.
6 I am following here the suggestion made by Aidan Nichols OP in his study of the Catechism, *The Splendour of Doctrine* (Edinburgh, 1995), pp. 66–7.
7 The passage from St John Eudes referred to at paragraph 521 is read in the Liturgy of the Hours, Office of Readings, for Friday of week 33.

8 For an example of this approach, Juan Luis Segundo, *The Historical Jesus of the Synoptics* (Maryknoll, NY, 1985).

9 Hans Urs von Balthasar, *Does Jesus Know Us? Do We Know Him?* (San Francisco, 1987), pp. 23–7: the emphasis is mine.

10 *Lumen Gentium* 5.

11 Two useful introductions to this theme are Geza Vermes, *Jesus the Jew* (London, 1973) and E. P. Sanders, *Jesus and Judaism* (London, 1985).

12 Sixth lesson from the Office of Tenebrae for Good Friday from the old Roman Breviary – my translation.

13 *Nostra Aetate* 4.

14 But some scholars would see in Jesus' challenge to the temple and its clergy the main reason for his arrest and execution: see Sanders, *Jesus and Judaism*, chapters 1 and 11.

15 Herbert McCabe, *God Matters* (London, 1987), p. 48.

16 Von Balthasar, *Mysterium Paschale*, p. 29.

17 Thomas Aquinas, *Summa Theol.* 3a.50.4.

18 Quoted in John Saward, *The Mysteries of March* (London, 1990), p. 129.

19 *Collected Poems of Charles Causley* (London, 1992), p. 57.

PART THREE

I believe in the Holy Spirit

THE CATECHISM'S TREATMENT of the last article of the Creed opens with a resoundingly trinitarian formula, which deserves quotation in full.

> 'No-one can say "Jesus is Lord" except by the Holy Spirit.'
> 'God has sent the Spirit of his Son into our hearts, crying
> "Abba! Father!" ' This knowledge of faith is possible only in
> the Holy Spirit: to be in touch with Christ, we must first have
> been touched by the Holy Spirit. He comes to meet us and
> kindles faith in us. By virtue of our Baptism, the first sacrament
> of the faith, the Holy Spirit in the Church communicates to us,
> intimately and personally, the life that originates in the Father
> and is offered to us in the Son. (683)

That splendid statement compresses most of the main themes of the Catechism's treatment of the Spirit – the Spirit is the gift of the Father, is inextricably linked to the work of the Son, and is the means by which we know, confess and share in the benefits of that work. The Spirit is the giver of faith, the life of the Church and of the individual believer, the animating principle in the sacraments. The Spirit, in short, is, as the Creed puts it, 'Lord and giver of life'.

The emergence, or rather the re-emergence, of so rich a doctrine of the Spirit in contemporary Catholicism is one of the most striking fruits of the Council. Catholicism has always had a rich *theology* of the Spirit as the third person of the Trinity, but in the later Middle Ages and after the Council of Trent its practical understanding of ways in which the Spirit worked and was present in the Church (there was even less reflection on the Spirit's presence in the *world*) tended to shrivel down to two main perceptions. The Spirit was thought of as the source of personal holiness, and as the guarantor of the infallibility and authority of the 'magisterium' or teaching office of the Church, above all of the Pope. This aspect of the Spirit's presence in the Church was even talked of as a 'continuing Incarnation', with a consequent tendency for the actions of the institutional Church to be identified with the actions of God, to became sacrosanct, unchallengeable: 'we never make mistakes'.

As a result, the sense that the Spirit is present not statically but dynamically in the Church, enlivening, refreshing and enabling every dimension of its life, including and even especially those aspects which did not come under formal structure and hierarchy, was almost lost. The great Dominican theologian Yves Congar, who played a crucial role in the Council, liked to tell the story of the theologian who complained to one of the authors of *Lumen Gentium* 'I see you talk about the Holy Spirit. Actually, you know, it's the Protestants who do that. We Catholics have the magisterium.'[1]

Catholics of course *experienced* the work of the Holy Spirit, and were well aware of the forces of life, joy and renewal which made up the vitality of the Church, but they tended to talk about these using different sorts of symbolism, and to link them to other aspects of the Christian mystery – to the Eucharist, to the figure of the Pope, above all to the Blessed Virgin Mary. Gerard Manley Hopkins' beautiful poem 'The Blessed Virgin Compared to the Air we Breathe' is full of the language of nurture, life-giving, spontaneity and renewal that we now recognize belongs properly to talk about the Spirit.

> Wild air, world mothering air,
> Nestling me everywhere . . .
> This needful, never-spent
> And nursing element;
> My more than meat and drink,
> My meal at every wink . . .
> If I have understood,
> She holds high motherhood

Towards all our ghostly good
And plays in grace her part
About man's beating heart ...[2]

In Catholic piety Mary was given titles which properly belong to the Spirit – Advocate, Consoler, Mediatrix, Wisdom. Such an identification of the figure of Mary with the work of the Spirit had its problems, but it also represented a profound insight. Much of the early Church's thinking about the Spirit was based on biblical passages concerned with the eternal Wisdom of God, a *feminine* figure, and as the type or icon of the Church Mary does indeed bring into focus much that we need to say about the work of the Spirit within redeemed humanity. In the words of an ancient Spanish prayer, much loved by Pope Paul VI:

> I pray to you, I pray to you, Holy Virgin: that I may receive Jesus myself from that Spirit who enabled you to conceive Jesus. May my soul receive Jesus through that Spirit who enabled your flesh to conceive that same Jesus ... May I love Jesus in that Spirit in whom you adore him yourself as your Lord and in whom you contemplate him as your Son.[3]

For the first thing to grasp about the Spirit is that, though the Church confesses him (or her?) as the third person of the Holy Trinity, in the case of the Spirit the notion of person is more than usually misleading. As the Catechism insists, 'the Spirit does not speak of himself', and 'we know him only in the movement by which he reveals the Word to us and disposes us to welcome him [Christ] in faith' (687). If God the Father is invisible because he is infinitely *other* than us, God the Holy Spirit is invisible because he is infinitely close to us, because he lives in our hearts. If we want to think of the Spirit in 'person' terms at all, we need to translate 'person' into 'people', we must think of him as the life *within* us, and within all things. The Spirit is real, a distinct and fundamental dimension of the life of God, but it is a reality we will only 'see' in the Kingdom, when all God's people have been gathered together in Christ. *What* we will see is not something or someone distinct from the human race, but the life and glory of God shining in their faces. The Spirit is *God's life being communicated to others*, because of the work of Christ, and for the completion and perfection of that work.

A book on the Holy Spirit published some years ago was entitled *The Go-Between God*. It's a helpful phrase, for the Spirit is the bond between redeemed humanity and God, and between human beings themselves: it is in the Spirit that we can make the leap of love and understanding that breaks down the barriers of sin and incomprehension. But we shouldn't imagine that the Spirit is a 'go-between' in the sense of someone who *comes between* us and God. He is not someone else, something extra, a third thing, in addition to the Father and the Son, or in addition to us and our neighbour. The Spirit is the *way* in which the Father and the Son come to us to transform us and share their life with us, he is the life of God within us.

Because she is life itself, the fundamental biblical image for the Spirit is *ruach, breath*, air, wind. The wind is invisible, free, unpredictable, blowing where it will, and bringing with it life and flourishing and refreshment. God's breath moves on the waters of creation, and Christ on the Cross in St John's gospel will 'give up his spirit' by breathing out his final breath. On Easter night he gives the Spirit to the apostles by breathing on them (691, 730), and in the pre-conciliar liturgy of the Easter Vigil the priest recalled all this by breathing three times on the waters of baptism as he called upon the Holy Spirit to sanctify it for new birth.

So the Catechism is concerned here not with the Spirit in himself, but in us and in creation, with the Spirit in action, and for that reason it relates all that it says about the Spirit to the life and sacraments of the Church. A very valuable section explores some of the principal symbols of the Holy Spirit, tracing them briefly from Scripture and linking them to the way in which they are used in the Church. Bafflingly, 'breath' is absent from this list – perhaps because, sadly, most of the powerful symbolic moments in the liturgy when the priest used breath as a sign of the Spirit's presence, like those at the Easter Vigil, have been removed. Despite that, this section,

with its firm rooting of doctrine in the worship and practice
of the Church, is very well adapted to practical catechesis.

The symbols discussed include water, anointing, fire, cloud
and light, the seal, the hand and finger, and the dove. In
every case these symbols of the Spirit are related to Christ –
the dove, for example, is the dove which descends on him at
his baptism, and in some churches (as in many English
churches before the Reformation) the Blessed Sacrament is
reserved in a hanging container shaped like a dove, thereby
underlining the role of the Spirit in bringing about the
presence of Christ in the Church and especially in the Eucharist, and in making that presence a living reality in our hearts.
(694–701)

As all this makes clear, the Catechism never separates the
work of the Spirit from the work of Christ, declaring that
theirs is a 'joint mission', and echoing the teaching of St
Irenaeus that Word and Spirit are the two hands of God in
creation (702–704). It sees this joint mission in three phases
– 'God's Spirit and Word in the time of promises' (before the
Incarnation) (702–716); 'The Spirit of Christ in the fullness
of time ' (the New Testament events) (717–730); and 'The
Spirit and the Church in the last days' (our present existence) (731–741).

God's Spirit and Word in the time of promises

The Spirit is Lord and giver of life: she is at work in creation
itself, and it is she who animates all that lives, all that is. The
Catechism devotes only a single paragraph to this tremendous truth (703), and does not develop it. Its teaching in this
whole section is concerned with the role of the Spirit in
salvation history, and it does not expand on the presence of
the Holy Spirit in creation at large. This wider presence,
however, deserves much fuller treatment. It offers the possibility of a positive assessment not only of the material world,
which is God's own work and which lives with his life, but also
of human culture and even religion outside the sphere of
Israel and the Church. The wisdom literature of the Old

Testament thought of God's Wisdom or Spirit as the creative life of God 'pervading and penetrating all things', playing a fundamental role in all the activities of the human spirit, anything in fact to which we might give the term 'inspired' – arts and sciences, government, morality, philosophy (Wisdom of Solomon 7:15 – 8:4). A sense of this cosmic activity of the Spirit in creation underlay the openness of the Council Fathers to the notion of a creative exchange between Church and World, and of the positive value of human achievement outside the Church.

This theological conviction that God is the source and meaning of all that is best in humanity is one of the major themes of *Gaudium et Spes*. Of course it has many problems, for, sloppily handled, it can lead to an uncritical endorsement of the current values of our society, to a loss of a sense of the unique value and necessity of revelation, and to forgetfulness of the inevitable tension which must exist in a fallen world between our human will and wisdom and the will and wisdom of God.

Nevertheless, there is here a great truth which needs exploring. Its other dimension, the sense of God as the life of the whole created world, has recurred again and again in Christian history, as a profound perception of the unity and harmony of all things in God. St Francis of Assisi's 'Canticle of the Creatures' is perhaps the best-known Christian expression of this vision of the whole natural world living by the life of God. It points, among other things, to the possibility of a Christian basis for contemporary ecological concerns.

Be praised, my Lord, by all your creatures,
and specially by our brother, Master Sun,
who brings the day to us,
you give us light through him:
how radiant and beautiful he is in all his splendour,
and so he speaks to us of you, O most high.

Be praised, my Lord, by the moon and by the stars,
which you have formed in the heavens,
bright and precious and lovely.

Be praised my Lord, by brothers wind and air,
by fair weather and by stormy, and by every season
through which you give sustenance to all that you have made.

Be praised, my lord, by sister water,
so very useful is she, so humble, precious, pure.

Be praised, my Lord, by brother fire,
through whom you brighten up the night:
how beautiful he is, how jolly, how powerful and strong.

Be praised, my Lord, through sister earth, our Mother,
who nourishes and rules us,
bringing forth fruits in their variety, and coloured flowers, and
herbs ...[4]

The Catechism's main focus, however, is the work of the Spirit in salvation history. The Creed declares that the Spirit 'has spoken through the prophets'. As God reveals himself in the history of Israel, it is the Spirit who opens the minds and hearts of the chosen people to God's promises. These promises culminate in the Messianic hope of the book of Isaiah, with its vision of one who will come and upon whom will rest 'the spirit of wisdom and understanding, the spirit of counsel and might, the spirit of knowledge and of fear of the Lord' (712; Isaiah 11:1–2). It was in the light of these prophecies that Jesus himself understood his own ministry, in which the outpouring of the Spirit would be directed especially towards the poor and downtrodden: in the synagogue at Nazareth he preached on the prophecies of Isaiah, declaring that he had been anointed 'to bring good tidings to the afflicted ... to bind up the broken hearted, to proclaim liberty to the captives' (714; Isaiah 61:1–2; Luke 4:18–19). The promises of the Spirit were promises for inner renewal, a 'new heart', and the raising up of a people 'poor' in heart and spirit, 'prepared for the Lord', was the 'hidden work' of the Spirit in Israel (716). One of the greatest hymns to the Holy Spirit, the *Veni Sancte Spiritus*, invokes the Spirit as *Pater pauperum*, father of the poor, and in a marvellous phrase Yves Congar spoke of the Spirit as 'the water which flows towards the lowest'.[5] The theme of the Spirit's special affinity with the poor runs through the whole of this section of the Catechism, and although the precise content and identity of the poor either in biblical times or now is (perhaps characteristically) not explored, there is much scope here for further reflection on the relationship between the mission of the Church and the poor in our own society.

The Spirit of Christ in the fullness of time

Turning to the Spirit in the New Testament, the Catechism focuses its discussion on three figures: John the Baptist, Mary, and Jesus himself.

John, Luke tells us, was 'filled with the Holy Spirit even from his mother's womb'. He prefigures the Spirit's work of declaring and making known what God will do in Jesus – he 'bears witness to the light'. He sums up in himself the prophetic tradition in which the Spirit's promises were declared, and as he baptizes Jesus the Spirit descends to anoint the Messiah for his ministry and his saving death. Finally, John's baptism prefigures the sacrament of baptism in which the Spirit makes us all children of God by a new birth (717–720).

Mary is 'the master-work of the mission of the Son and the Spirit in the fullness of time'. In her the Father finds the 'dwelling-place' where the Son and the Spirit can dwell among men. She is thus called by the Church 'Seat of Wisdom' (721). There is a good deal of compressed theology in these claims, which the Catechism does not really unpack. In Luke's story of the Annunciation the angel tells Mary that the Holy Spirit will 'overshadow' her. The word he uses here comes from the Greek version of the Old Testament and is used to describe the descent of the 'Shekinah' or glory of God, in the form of a burning cloud, on to the Tent of Meeting. In the Tent was placed the Ark of the Covenant, basically a sacred box with carrying handles in which were placed the Ten Commandments, and which was believed to be God's throne or footstool. There God came to speak with Moses, and there he 'camped out ' or 'tabernacled' with his people in the desert.[6] St John draws on this same cluster of images when he tells us that the Word 'tabernacled' amongst us (though we tend to translate the Greek 'dwelt amongst us'). There is a special profundity in the fact that we call the place where the Blessed Sacrament is kept not a 'house', but a 'tabernacle' or tent, where God, now as in ancient Israel and in the Incarnation, comes not to settle down, but to meet us as companion and support upon our journey through the wilderness.

So Mary is the new Tent of Meeting, and the new Ark of the Covenant. In her womb, by the overshadowing of the Spirit, is formed the child who will become the new meeting-place of heaven and earth. He is God's Wisdom itself, and, in her womb and on her lap, she is his living throne. The Litany of Our Lady (the Litany of Loreto) calls her 'Ark of the Covenant', and 'Seat of Wisdom', and it is as the throne of the Wisdom of God, her child in her lap, that she is often portrayed: the pilgrimage statue at Walsingham is a representation of Mary as Seat of Wisdom. In this role she makes visible her son, to the Gentiles in the persons of the Magi, but above all to the poor and humble, to those who long and wait for the promises of God – the shepherds, Simeon, Anna. Mary's special role in the work of the Spirit in the new creation is manifested by her presence with the apostles at Pentecost (721–726).

All this reaches its climax in the person of Christ Jesus himself. His whole work 'is in fact a joint mission of the Son and the Holy Spirit', and the Catechism emphasizes that everything which is said of Jesus must be understood in the light of and in association with the work of the Spirit. Anointed with the Spirit, Christ in his ministry promises to pour that Spirit out on his disciples. In St John's gospel in particular this association between Jesus and the Spirit is explored. Christ is our Counsellor and Comforter: the Spirit will be the other Comforter, continuing Christ's presence amongst us (we can even speak of the Spirit as 'Vicar of Christ'), and bringing the world to a knowledge of its own sin, of judgement and of redemption. On the Cross Christ releases his Spirit, and from that hour the mission of Christ and the Spirit becomes the mission of the Church – 'as the Father sends me, so I send you' (730).

The Spirit and the Church in the last days

Pentecost is the reversal of Babel: in place of pride, hostility, and a cacophony of unintelligible speech which make understanding impossible, God gives healing, unity, love, communication. God *is* love, and his first and best gift is love, containing all others. As Paul says, 'God's love has been poured into our hearts through the Holy Spirit who has been given to us' (733; Romans 5:5). The first effect of this love is the forgiveness of sins, restoring to us the lost image of God. We become God's children, and are given the pledge of our future glory in God himself: the gifts of the Spirit are the first-fruits of our final destiny – love, joy, peace, patience, kindness, goodness, faithfulness, gentleness, self-control. This life in the Spirit is the life of the Church, which is the body of Christ and the temple of the Spirit. In the Church's Eucharist this life has its focus: there, by the power of the Spirit the risen Lord is made manifest, human beings are reconciled to God and one another, and brought into true communion. The Church is therefore the sacrament of the mission of Christ and the Holy Spirit, it exists to announce, bear witness to and make present the life of the Holy Trinity in the world. In its sacraments it shares in Christ's self-offering and the outpouring of the life of the Spirit; in the living out of the will of God and the life of the virtues, the fruits of the Spirit and the new creation manifest themselves, and in prayer the Spirit himself intercedes for us. These three dimensions of the work of the Spirit – the sacraments, the pursuit of a holy life, and the practice of prayer, will form the basis for the other three sections of the Catechism (739–741).

•

The Catechism's section on the Church is immensely long, nearly two hundred paragraphs, far longer than its treatment of the Holy Spirit. Yet it is intended essentially as a sub-section of what it has to say about the Spirit. The authors remind us that we believe in God, Father, Son and Holy Spirit, but we do not in the same way 'believe in' the Church, for the Church in itself is not an object of faith – we are not to confuse God with his works, and we must realize that all that the Church has is the gift of God (750). The gift of God is, supremely, the Spirit, and so 'the article concerning the Church ... depends entirely on the article about the Holy Spirit' (749).

The Church and the Spirit

This immediately gives us a measure to assess the Catechism's teaching on the Church: how far does it embody a properly balanced sense of the Church as the instrument and expression of the life of the Spirit? Some of the Orthodox observers at the Second Vatican Council thought that a document on the Church need have only two chapters – one on the Spirit, and one on the experience of the Christian life; some remained convinced that even after the Council the Catholic Church remained too preoccupied with hierarchy and structure, the mere nuts and bolts of the Church's life. In fact, the Council's teaching on the Church was profoundly influenced by its doctrine of the Holy Spirit, and the Catechism's task here is to interpret faithfully that teaching. Cardinal Yves Congar has suggested some criteria for assessing such a 'Spirit-based' theology of the Church, which will help us get our bearings on what the Catechism has to say.[7]

For Congar, any sound understanding of the Church as part of the action of the Holy Spirit must have five essential marks. Firstly, it must recognize that the Church is not complete, ready-made, self-contained. The Spirit's presence within it to bring Christ to birth means that the Church is constantly being renewed, constantly being moulded and shaped by God. There is therefore room for all the faithful to share in this ongoing work, to 'bear and exercise their creativity' within it. Secondly, the fullness of the Spirit in the Church comprises the sum total of the gifts which the Spirit has showered on it. These gifts include the individual charisms or talents which have been bestowed on lay people as well as clergy. The Church is not a pyramid, with a passive and docile laity at the bottom, taking orders from the Pope, bishops and clergy at the top. This fullness also includes the gifts found within local and regional churches as well as individuals. The catholicity of the Church, its fullness, consists not in some artificially imposed uniformity, like a chain of out-of-town superstores, every one exactly the same, but in its possession of the full range and diversity of gifts which the Spirit pours out on humanity. Indeed, in a sense Catholicism *is* diversity. What makes all this catholic, and not chaos, is the holding together of this diversity not in military discipline, but true communion. It is not rules and structures which make the Church one: the living Spirit of the Lord, who is love, 'holds all things together' (Wisdom of Solomon 1:7).

Yet love, too, needs structure, and this leads us to the third mark of a sound understanding of the Church, which is a recognition of order within diversity. The charisms of the Spirit are many, and range from ordinary natural gifts like administrative or financial ability, through ecclesial gifts like preaching or theological discernment, to extraordinary gifts like those of healing or prophecy. All are given for the good of the Church, and must therefore be brought into relation with the other gifts and charisms present in the Church. All these gifts may lead to forms of ministry, and the Council spoke of the 'right and duty' of the faithful to exercise their charisms within the Church (*Apostolicam Actuositatem* 3). In this process, the ordained ministry, and in particular the bishops, have a special, God-given role of discernment and government. This role is not over against and separate from the other charisms present in the Church, but it is their special responsibility, the sacramental expression of the Spirit's 'ordering' of the Church.

Congar's fourth mark is that the doctrine of the Church should be trinitarian. By this he means particularly that the unity of the Church should reflect the communion of persons within God, marked by diversity, yet also by mutual communication and exchange. So we must not get tied up in notions of hierarchy which present the action of the Spirit as coming in one direction only, for example from the top down.

Finally, our doctrine of the Church must be marked by openness to the future: while remaining faithful to and using the gifts that God has given in the past, we must relate what has already been received from Christ to what is still to come. In St John's gospel Christ promises that 'When the Spirit of truth comes, he will guide you into all the truth ... he will declare to you the things that are to come'. We live in that epoch of unfolding, looking for the fulfilment of God's will for his Church and his world. So our understanding of the Church must make us receptive to what Pope John and the Council called 'the signs of the times', ready to greet and forward the work of God wherever we find it. For Congar that will point us beyond the Church, outwards to the 'profane' world, and he quotes the saying of Ambrosiaster, 'Every true thing, whoever may utter it, is from the Holy Spirit'.

On the whole, the Catechism's teaching on the Church measures up well to most if not quite all of these criteria. It is true that this whole section of the Catechism is somewhat constrained by the way in which it has been put together. A glance at the footnotes will show that, to a far greater extent than most other sections, this is a 'scissors and paste' job, drawing very heavily on the Council's Constitution on the Church, *Lumen Gentium*, and, to a lesser extent, on the conciliar documents on the Laity and on Ecumenism, while the final part, dealing with the religious life, threatens to degenerate into a series of desperately dry extracts from the Code of Canon Law. The dependence on *Lumen Gentium* was both inevitable and right: it represents the high-point of the Council's teaching, and transformed the understanding and experience of the Church for most Catholics. The Catechism's main concern, therefore, is to mediate that teaching within the overall framework of a discussion of the Creed, and in that, despite its sometimes dry presentation, it largely succeeds. The distinctive characteristics of *Lumen Gentium* – its subordination of the institutional and hierarchical dimension of the Church to a sense of its sacramental character as the sign and instrument of Christ's presence in the world, its emphasis on the pilgrim and provisional character of the Church's present forms, its recovery of a sense of the dignity and responsibility of the whole people of God, not just the clergy, and its location of Christian ministry within a context of mutual responsibility and service – all these are clearly set out in the Catechism. Hints of an older, more military sense of hierarchy persist – in an unfortunate quotation from Pope Pius XII which evokes the Church as a sort of army, the laity at the front line, under the leadership of the Pope (899), or a passage in which the members of a bishop's diocese are described as 'his subjects' (896)! But these are uncharacteristic lapses in a discussion which overall conveys well the fundamental positions of the Council. It is true, however, that the insights of *Lumen Gentium* and of the document on Ecumenism, *Unitatis Redintegratio*, are not much developed here, and the thirty years of ecumenical activity since the Council is hardly reflected at all in these pages – nothing is incorporated, for example, from the very important theological work of ARCIC. More significantly, and perhaps more justifiably, the Catechism's handling of the notion of 'openness to the world', represented by the Council's Pastoral Constitution, *Gaudium et Spes*, suggests that its authors share some of the reservations about *Gaudium et Spes* which surfaced during the Council itself, and which have gained support at the centre of the Church since then.

The Church's origin, foundation and mission

From the start, the Catechism meets one of Congar's most important criteria by setting its teaching on the Church firmly within a trinitarian framework. The Church was born of the Father's heart, instituted by Christ Jesus, and revealed by the Holy Spirit. The Church is the expression of the eternal love for us which exists in the heart of God, and it is the 'calling together' of human beings into a marvellous communion of love (748–752). We can therefore say, as the early Christians did, that the world 'was created for the sake of the Church', for the world exists so that all creatures might share the life of God. Prepared for in the calling of Israel, and in the longings in the hearts of all humanity, the Church is 'the goal of all things' (758–762). In the fullness of time Christ, proclaiming the inauguration of the Kingdom of God, established the Church on the foundation of the twelve apostles, as a new Israel. The Church, however, is not a mere *organization*, formed to promote Jesus' objectives. It is the sacrament of his self-giving, anticipated in the Eucharist and completed on the Cross. The Church's eternal origins in the heart of the Father are reflected in the scriptural moment of its beginning: it is born from the pierced heart of Christ hanging dead on the Cross (763–766). At Pentecost this Church is revealed, endowed with the gifts of the Spirit, and given the mission to make disciples of all nations. Journeying as a pilgrim through persecution and consolation, she will be united in glory with her Lord at the end of time (767–769).

In all this the Catechism studiously avoids merely functional language about the Church, and concentrates on its spiritual role and destiny in God's plan. There is more to this than just an attempt to mirror the teaching of *Lumen Gentium*: what we have here is a reflection of the unease which has grown up since the Council, particularly but by no means exclusively in Vatican circles, about the 'politicizing' of Catholic thinking about the Church. Von Balthasar once complained that the Church had 'to a large extent put off its mystical characteristics; it has become a church of permanent

conversations, organisations, advisory commissions, congres-
ses, synods, academies, parties, pressure-groups, functions,
structures and restructurings, sociological experiments, sta-
tistics: that is to say, more than ever a male Church'.[8]
Von Balthasar's language, and the assumptions it makes
about the inherent characteristics of women, will not delight
every feminist, and it can be pressed into service to bolster the
unaccountable use of authority. It has been echoed in more
than one Vatican directive, and we need to beware when
those who exercise power within the Church tell us we should
not bother our little heads about questions of responsibility,
power, accountability. Yet von Balthasar was making a valid
and very necessary theological point. The Church is not a
pressure group or a party, it is a sacrament of the unity which
God wills for the whole of humanity, and we need to attend to
its value as sign, promise, community of gift, before we
concern ourselves with structures.

This the Catechism does in its consideration of 'the mystery of the Church' (the theme and title of the first chapter of
Lumen Gentium). The Church as mystery has two dimensions.
It is 'mystery', in the first place, because its dignity, holiness
and destiny are hidden under its institutional and historical
exterior, sinful and mortal as they are: the Church, in St
Bernard's words, is both 'body of death and temple of light'
(771). It is 'mystery' in the second place because it is a
sacrament – the sacrament of humanity's union with God,
and of our union with each other, the 'universal sacrament of
redemption'. The Church is the place of holiness, loved by
God, and drawing all humanity into the love of God. This
relationship with Christ is like that of bride and groom. The
bridal character of the Church is summed up by the Catechism as the 'Marian dimension' of the Church, an idea
embodied in the eighth chapter of *Lumen Gentium*, though in
fleshing out that idea here the Catechism is once again
following the distinctive teaching of Hans Urs von Balthasar.
For von Balthasar it is the 'bridal', 'Marian', feminine, dimension of the Church which is its most fundamental and definitive characteristic, the dimension which is concerned with

love, fidelity, trust, with the nourishing of believers, but also with suffering alongside Christ, as Mary did at Calvary, and bringing forth children in a sorrow born of love. This 'Marian' dimension is not concerned with function, but with the giving and receiving of love, with trust, patience, being. Von Balthasar contrasted the Marian dimension with the Petrine dimension, which is organizational, didactic, activist: the Church needs both, but in the order of grace the Marian dimension takes precedence; indeed, he pointed out that on Good Friday only the Marian dimension of the Church existed, for the apostles had all run away.[9] And so the Catechism declares that 'the Marian dimension of the Church precedes the Petrine' (773). It thereby warns us against too functionalist and hierarchical an understanding of the Church. Yet the Church is also an 'instrument', the means by which God calls human beings into unity with himself and with each other. Characteristically, the Catechism does not descend to specifics, to spell out the wider implications of this idea, or how the sacramental unity of people within the Church relates to the social structures and forms of human community outside the Church. There is scope here for further development of these ideas (774–776).

The Church: People of God, Body of Christ, Temple of the Spirit

Once again adopting a trinitarian structure, the Catechism now moves on to consider the Church as the People of God, as the Body of Christ, and as the Temple of the Holy Spirit. The Second Vatican Council chose the notion of the People of God as its key title for the Church. It was a decision which was controversial at the time, and which even some of the theologians whose work had done most to prepare for the Council, such as Cardinal Henri de Lubac, had reservations about.[10] Since the Council, some have feared that the concept of the 'People of God' has given rise to an inappropriately democratic or quasi-political way of thinking within the Church, and so to agitation for lay rights, greater representation, ordination of women, and so on. There were therefore some fears that the concept of the People of God might be marginalized in the Catechism. In fact it is given a prominent place, and the overall thrust of the Council's teaching under this heading is faithfully reflected in what the Catechism has to say. This people share Christ's office as priest, prophet and king. As priests they consecrate the whole of human activity to God, as prophets they share in the preaching and preservation of the faith, as kings they help transform the structures of the world into accordance with the rule of Christ, and they also share in the ministries of the Church. All these dimensions are developed at a later point in the Catechism's discussion, when it considers the role of lay people in the Church (see 897–913).

The themes which the Council introduced under the heading of the People of God – the dignity and responsibility of the whole priestly people, and the diversity within unity which exists in Christ, are developed under the two following headings of the Body of Christ and the Temple of the Holy Spirit – a move from the 'political' to the biological and cultic or sacral, designed no doubt to offset the disruptive potential of the 'people' theme. As we would expect from Congar's criteria for a 'Spirit-based' ecclesiology, this section emphasizes both the vital, energizing presence of the Spirit in the Church, building it up in love and bringing growth and healing through the sacraments, and the presence within the Church of ordinary and extraordinary charisms, 'a wonderfully rich grace for the apostolic vitality and for the holiness of the entire Body of Christ'.

There is, however, a detectable note of constraint at this point : the exercise of these charisms is to be regulated by charity, which is fair enough, and none is exempt 'from being referred and submitted to the Church's shepherds'. The wording here is noticeably more restrictive and nervous than the corresponding passage of the Council's declaration on the role of the laity. This did indeed say that it was for the pastors to 'pass judgement on the authenticity and good use of these gifts', but only after emphasizing the right of those who possess them to exercise them 'in the freedom of the

Holy Spirit who breathes where he wills', a 'charismatic' emphasis that the Catechism tones down (*Apostolicam Actuositatem* 3). Nevertheless, the essential point is made that charisms carry not only their own blessing, but their own authority – 'Charisms are to be accepted with gratitude by the person who receives them, and by all the members of the Church as well' (799–801).

One, holy, catholic, apostolic

Having established this broad base for its doctrine of the Church, in which the institutional dimension of the Church is firmly subordinated to its trinitarian, spiritual and communal character, the Catechism turns to consider the four traditional 'marks' of the Church – unity, holiness, catholicity, and apostolicity. Once again, the features which Congar saw as essential for a sound 'Spirit-based' doctrine of the Church are well in evidence. This can be seen most clearly in the section on unity (813–822).

The unity of the Church before the Council was often conceived of in monolithic, quasi-military terms, laying great emphasis on uniformity of liturgy and especially the universal celebration of the Mass and other sacraments in Latin, on strict discipline, and even the suppression of different styles and emphases in theology. Many of the theologians whose work was most crucial for the Council, like Congar and de Lubac (both later Cardinals), had been silenced at one time or another in the reign (that seems the right word in this context) of Pope Pius XII, and Congar had even been sent into what he thought of as the Gulag exile of Cambridge for a year. There were ecumenical implications in all this, for of course such a heavy emphasis on uniformity meant that Christians outside the visible unity of the Roman Catholic Church were assumed to be also altogether outside the Body of Christ, their clergy mere laymen, their sacraments absolutely null and utterly void.

The Council brought renewal in all these areas, and its emphases are duly reflected in the Catechism. At the very start of its discussion it had located the meaning and identity of the Church not solely in the worldwide communion of believers, the international body presided over by the Pope, we normally describe as the Catholic Church, but in the liturgical assembly and in the local community . The Church is a communion of churches (752, 833–834). The unity of the Church here is seen not as monolithic but as rooted in the life of the Trinity, a unity of persons, which encompasses 'a multiplicity of peoples and cultures'. From the beginning the Church's unity has been marked by 'a great diversity which comes from both the variety of God's gifts and the diversity of those who receive them'. This diversity includes 'particular Churches which retain their own traditions', and far from damaging unity this difference of traditions brings 'great richness' (813–814). Held together in the bond of love and by the visible links of a common faith received from the apostles, the shared celebration of the sacraments, and the apostolic succession through the sacrament of holy orders, the one Church 'subsists in' the Roman Catholic Church.

This phrase 'subsists in' was one of the Council's crucial contributions to thinking about the unity of the Church. The Council deliberately refrained from saying that the Roman Catholic Church simply *was* the one true Church. The phrase 'subsists in', while maintaining that the fullness of catholic unity was to be found within the visible (Roman Catholic) Church, opened the way to acknowledging that other churches too might share, in greater or lesser degrees, in the mystery of the one Church. The phrase has provoked a mountain of paper and endless speculation about its precise implications, but its retention here is an important act of faithfulness to the Council's thinking.

So the Catechism recognizes that Christian disunity is a fact arising from sin, but that responsibility for disunity is shared. It welcomes as brothers and sisters all the baptized, and recognizes that in their churches are to be found many elements of Catholic faith and practice. So the separated churches and 'ecclesial communities' are no mere associations of individual Christians, but divinely graced 'means of salvation'. Within all the elements of catholic truth shared by the churches the Catechism recognizes an inbuilt dynamic towards unity, and the search for unity is seen both as a gift given by Christ, and an obligation laid on the Church, 'the call of the Holy Spirit' (820–821).

The section on the catholicity of the Church, one of the richest in this part of the Catechism, shows some signs of the tensions which have arisen within the Church since the Council over the issue of openness, to the future and to the world, the questions which are touched on in Congar's fifth criterion for a 'Spirit-based' ecclesiology. 'Catholic' means universal, or whole, and the Church's fundamental catholicity is two-fold. It is rooted in its fullness as the Body of Christ – 'the Church is catholic because Christ is present in her', who is the fullness of God – and because it has been sent on a mission to the whole human race.

Who belongs to this Catholic Church? Indeed, if the Church is truly the 'universal sacrament of salvation', the *sign* of the unity God wills for all people, then in some sense that unity already exists, and the question might be better put, who does *not* belong to it? Following the lead of the Council, the Catechism presents us with a widening series of concentric circles, which ultimately includes all human beings of good will. Most obviously, the Church is made up of those in the visible communion of the Catholic Church. Beyond this circle, are the other churches and ecclesial communities sharing to a greater or lesser degree in the one faith and in the sacraments. Beyond the other churches, the circles widen out, with a special place for the other children of Abraham, the Jews and Muslims. The Jews in particular, as the first to hear the Word of God, retain a special claim on God, whose gifts 'are irrevocable' (840–841). The Church recognizes also in the other religions a search 'among shadows and images' for the unknown God, and acknowledges in all that is good in them a preparation for the Gospel.

All this raises the question of why the Church is needed at all, and in what the uniqueness of Christ consists. In the aftermath of the Council there was indeed something of a collapse of confidence in the very idea of mission and conversion. The recognition of the presence of God in other cultures and religions, and the teaching of *Gaudium et Spes* on the need for the Church to display 'openness to the world', led to questionings of the uniqueness or necessity of the Christian way. Christians are and always have been a minority of the human race. What was the relationship of this minority to the non-Christian whole, what was God's will for those who were not Christian? Christians in the past were often profoundly pessimistic about the salvation of those outside the Church: the image of the Church as Noah's ark, invoked in the old Easter liturgy and recalled here by the Catechism (845), seemed to imply that salvation was limited to the baptized few. Nor can any modern theology, however well-intentioned, afford to discount the element of opposition and resistance to the Word of God which is a fundamental characteristic of the world. The Gospel is, inescapably, a call to costly conversion. To assume lightly the salvation of all is to belittle the depth of suffering and alienation in Christ's Passion, the price of reconciliation.

These questions are by no means new. They were already being discussed before the Council,[11] and they have continued to exercise theologians since. The Catechism's position on these issues is sensitive to the new emphases, though essentially traditional. The fundamental form of the Church's openness to the world is mission, for the Church is by nature a reflection of the mission of the Son and the Spirit, in eternity and in the world, and its task is to gather all humanity into the the love of God. The Church is 'the place where humanity must rediscover its unity and salvation', 'the world reconciled'. Accepting that God can and does save those who through no fault of their own are ignorant of the

gospel, the Catechism nevertheless recognizes in the goodness and truth found outside the Church not an end in itself
but 'a preparation for the Gospel', and it emphasizes the
commitment of the Church to the proclamation of the truth
of God (843, 849–856).

It envisages mission, however, a good deal more sensitively
than some past and present Western notions of mission,
which have often involved contempt for and even the ob-
literation of pagan culture. Mission is costly, a following of
the way of the Cross, and must accommodate readiness to
fail. It involves both the task of 'inculturation', enabling the
Gospel 'to take flesh in each people's culture', and it involves
a 'respectful dialogue' with those who do not yet accept the
Gospel, in which the Church must be open to 'those elements of truth and grace which are found among peoples
and which are, as it were, a secret presence of God' (856).
This emphasis, in this case derived from the Council's document on Mission, *Ad Gentes*, has obvious relevance to the
whole question of the presence of God in non-Christian
culture, and might well have been drawn into a discussion of
the question of salvation outside the Church.

What one misses throughout this discussion is a sense of
the role of the Church acting *on behalf* of humanity, as a
community which spells out what the whole of humanity
must attempt to live. We must take seriously the sacramental-
ity of the Church, as sign of an existing reality. There is a
sense in which it may be that the priestly role of the Church
may be carried out vicariously on behalf of the rest of humanity – we tend the altars so that blessing may fall elsewhere.
Moreover, mission is seen here too exclusively in terms of
rescue, of saving the rest of the world. There is no discussion
of the drive to mission as one in which we invite the world to
recognize and to praise the God already at work in its own
experience, summoning the world not to an entirely new
experience of God, but to a recognition, naming and giving
thanks for the force of creation and new creation which is
everywhere bringing God to birth.

Christ's faithful – hierarchy, laity, consecrated life

It is only at this late point in the discussion of the Church that the Catechism turns at last to questions of structure, order and hierarchy, and then only in the overall context of a discussion of all the faithful, in which emphasis is laid on a 'true equality with regard to dignity and activity' among Christians, clerical or lay. We should not look here for a developed theology of ordained ministry – that is reserved for treatment in the section on the sacraments. Instead, the Catechism at this point seeks to locate ordained ministry – in particular the episcopate – within the overall context of the charisms present among the people of God.

In this 'integral' account of the ministry, ordination is seen as the necessary authorization and empowerment of individuals by the whole body for the task of preaching and sanctifying. No-one can send themselves to preach the Gospel, no-one has a right to speak for Christ. Those so empowered are ordained into a ministry which is both personal – the form of their own discipleship – and collegial, an exercise of care for the whole Church which is localized in their own particular Church, but is an expression of the fraternal communion of all the faithful. Every bishop is at once a bishop of a local church, and of the whole communion of the Church. This wider communion, and the shared responsibility it entails, is maintained through the communion of each bishop with the bishop of the church at Rome, who inherits the Petrine ministry of confirming his brethren.

This section of the Catechism's exposition is very striking for its strong emphasis on the shared responsibility of the episcopate, 'collegiality'. The primacy and prerogatives of the Pope as head of the college of bishops and indispensable centre of unity are clearly set out, but not at the expense of the authority and responsibility of the rest of the bishops. Collegiality is a notion which has come a long way since the early days of the Council, when conservatives like Cardinal Ottaviani liked to claim that the only collegial action of the apostles was when they all abandoned the Lord before his

Passion! Nevertheless, it is a concept which has come under pressure recently, being seen by many as a concept which erodes the place of the Pope. A recent exchange between the Cardinal Archbishop of Armagh and the Bishop of Ferns made it clear that for the cardinal at any rate collegiality meant that no bishop must ever publicly disagree with the Pope. So it is all the more striking to see a strong doctrine of collegiality so uncompromisingly affirmed here. Even the exercise of papal infallibility is explained as an exercise of the teaching office which belongs to all the bishops, and the Pope in exercising it is spoken of as 'head of the college of bishops' (891).

The discussion of the role of the laity which follows recapitulates and expands the themes laid out earlier in the section on the people of God. This is the place in which the role of charisms in the Church receives its fullest treatment, and the Catechism emphasizes not only the role of lay people in consecrating and shaping the secular world, but their legitimate involvement as priests, prophets and kings in the life of the Church itself, in liturgy, teaching, theology, and the exercise of rule within the Church. The chapter concludes with a section on the consecrated life, largely drawn from the Code of Canon Law, but summed up in a passage from *Lumen Gentium* on the prophetic witness of the consecrated life 'that the world cannot be transfigured and offered to God without the spirit of the Beatitudes' (932).

The communion of saints

At its root, the Church is the sign of the unity of all things in Christ, and so the Catechism concludes its discussion of the Church with a reflection on this unity, 'the communion of saints'. In Eastern celebrations of the Eucharist, the Lord's Body and Blood are presented to the people by the celebrant with the proclamation *Sancta sanctis* – 'holy things for holy people'. There is of course a tension in the use of 'holy' here, for we come to the holy gifts of God as sinners: the Church is called holy not because it is full of good people, or because as an institution it is blameless and wholly beneficial, but because it is the place set apart by God to transform what is sinful into what is holy. To claim that the Church is holy, says St Augustine,

> is not to be understood as if the Church were like this already, but in the sense that it is being prepared to be like this, when [like Christ] it also will appear in glory. Now, because of the ignorance and weakness of its members, the whole Church must say every day 'forgive us our trespasses'.[12]

To belong to the Church is to be given a share in that movement towards the holy, to share 'holy things' with other sinners, who are nevertheless God's saints. The 'communion of saints' points us to our shared faith in God, to our shared life in the sacraments, to our sharing in the charisms and gifts which the Spirit pours out on the Church, and beyond and through them, to a shared life in charity, in which we care for one another, just as the first Christians 'had everything in common' (949–953).

But the communion of the Church extends beyond all this. For us, the ultimate breakdown of communion is death: it is the last unending silence and loneliness into which we must all come. In Christ, that solitude is abolished, and for those who believe, death is no longer the end of community, but the entry into a deeper communion of all the living and the dead. We share a single hope and a single redemption with the dead, a hope expressed in prayer. The triumphant dead, the saints, support us with their prayers in heaven, and we in our turn support those of the dead who, like us, remain *in via*, as pilgrims in need of healing and forgiveness, in purgatory, yet yearning towards our hope and fulfilment in Christ (954–958). The 'icon' of this unity in hope of all God's people is Mary: her resurrection, which we in the West call her Assumption, is the pledge of the destiny of the whole Church, 'the image and beginning of the Church as it is to be perfected in the world to come' (972).

It has to be said that this final passage on the role and status of Mary, the third extended treatment of her role in this part of the Catechism, though heavily dependent on *Lumen Gentium*, is not perfectly in harmony with the Council's presentation of her. The Council located its teaching on Mary within the document on the Church as a deliberate redirection of Marian piety and theology. Baroque devotion to Mary had placed her on a pedestal over against and above the Church, but the Council sought to reintegrate her as one of the redeemed, the icon and pattern for the Church and her fellow-believers. There was a counter-movement within the Council, which saw this as a reduction of Mary's status, and one of the symbols of this struggle was the attempt to define and clarify her privileges and titles: one of these contested titles was 'Mother of the Church', and among those opposed to its use was the young Joseph Ratzinger, later Cardinal Prefect of the Congregation for the Doctrine of the Faith, the Vatican's watch-dog of orthodoxy.[13] In the event, the Council declined to use this title, for it seemed to blur the fact that Mary was herself a member of the Church, though its most exalted and privileged member. After the Council, however, Pope Paul VI used this title in his very fine apostolic instruction on the place of Mary, *Marialis Cultus*: from there it was adopted into wider currency in the Church, and it is adopted as her title here. Mary's maternal status for Christians, of course, is an ancient and venerable theme of Catholic theology and devotion, but it is better, and more in line with the teaching of the Council, to think of her as Mother *in* the Church than as Mother *of* the Church, a role which properly belongs to the Holy Spirit.

I BELIEVE IN THE RESURRECTION OF THE BODY, AND LIFE EVERLASTING

With the last article of the Creed, the Catechism turns to consider the ultimate enigma, the mystery of death, and the hope of resurrection. In doing so, it invites us to consider Christianity at its most uncompromising, for even in the

ancient world, as a quotation from St Augustine here witnesses, 'On no point does the Christian faith encounter more
opposition than on the resurrection of the body' (996).

Death is that which undoes us, the nothing into which
everything living falls. For the animal and plant world it is a
part of the natural process, and for human beings too it can
be a poignant but accepted part of life. Death, as the Catechism says, is the 'natural end of life', and our mortality can
serve to make life itself more precious and more weighty, it
'lends urgency to our lives' (1007). Yet for us humans, death
has another and more terrible dimension, which the Church
expresses in her belief that in some mysterious sense, death is
the consequence of sin (1008). Though individual deaths
may be natural, even a blessing, we experience mortality in
itself as the last enemy, the terrifying embodiment of all the
forces that diminish and destroy us: we all understand Dylan
Thomas's plea to his dying father

> Do not go gentle into that good night,
> Rage, rage against the dying of the light.

Death is the dark night which is the sacrament of our distance
from God, and from each other, the ultimate loneliness. And
so we resist and reject it. In his novel *Pincher Martin* William
Golding tells the story of a sailor shipwrecked on an Atlantic
rock, desperately resisting death, the 'black lightening' which
threatens 'the centre', Pincher Martin's consciousness. As
the story unfolds we come to realize that Martin's desperate
clinging to life, at the price of the appalling loneliness and
deprivation of his rock, is the expression of an inner desolation, his systematic and lifelong crushing of love and the
pursuit of his own ego at the expense of others. His inability
to die, to accept the 'black lightening', is the expression of his
inability to live.

It was by descending willingly into that desolation that
Christ redeemed us. For us death is constraint, we are bound
and taken where we do not want to go. Christ alone was 'free
among the dead', and 'the obedience of Jesus has transformed the curse of death into a blessing'. So at the heart of

our faith is the belief that, beyond hope or expectation, death 'has a positive meaning' (1009–1010). By sharing in Christ's dying, we enter into the new life he has found with God. For the Christian, death is not something that *happens* to us, a calamity, but something which, in union with Christ, we *do*, an offering to the Father. We can and should prepare for it, and the Catechism, with a profoundly Christian instinct, points us to the many traditional preparations for death, like the litany of the saints, which symbolize the tremendous reality that for us death is no longer the ultimate isolation. We do not die alone, we die into the communion of the redeemed. Death becomes the gateway of life, and St Francis ended his ecstatic celebration of all that lives, the 'Canticle of the Creatures', with a hymn of praise to death (1014).

The Christian hope in death is not for survival, but for resurrection, a share in the exalted human life that Christ now lives in God. As we have already seen in considering his Resurrection, that life is both human and yet unimaginably other: it belongs not to this world but to the end of the ages, the life of the world to come. Once we die, we are finished with time and the things of this world, for death is 'the end of man's earthly pilgrimage': there is no reincarnation, and our resurrection is in no sense a re-run of earthly existence (1013). And yet it is the resurrection of the body. It is what we do and are in this life which is transfigured and redeemed, nothing that is of God in us will be lost, though what that redemption means 'exceeds our imagination and under-standing' (1000). To help us make sense of this, the Cate-chism points us not to speculations about the afterlife or pictures of heaven, but to our experience within the Church, to the Mass. Our sharing in the Eucharist helps us to under-stand how these mortal bodies and earthly lives of ours can become the vehicles of eternal life. In the sacraments we already die with Christ and already, here and now, we live resurrection lives (1003). So whatever else the mysterious and wonderful doctrine of the resurrection of the body means, it fills our present lives with dignity and hope, it reveals that all that we are and do is infinitely precious and enduring in God's sight, it teaches us that our lives now matter to God eternally. Above all, it assures us that in the place we most fear, in the grave of all our hopes and longings, in death itself, we will encounter beyond destruction and nothingness, the endless and life-giving love of God.

After death, judgement. That is not a temporal sequence, for when we die there is an end of time: we are finished with before and after. To say that judgement comes *after* death is to say that there will then be no more decision-making for or against God: what matters, what will determine who and what we are for all eternity, is now. So all Christian teaching about judgement is teaching about the here and now : it calls us to conversion, commits us to 'the justice of the Kingdom of God', and proclaims our hope for the Lord's return. To believe in the final judgement, too, is to grasp the deadly seriousness of the choices we are given in life. It *matters* whether or not we respond to God: if we accept his grace and open ourselves to the love of Father, Son and Spirit, we will live with Christ in that love.

But refusal is also a possibility. Again and again Christ used the imagery of the rubbish dump and the bonfire to convey this terrible possibility. (His language, it should be noted, was figurative and not literal. 'Gehenna', as the Catechism ought to tell us but does not, was a rubbish tip and burning-place in a ravine outside Jerusalem.) Hell is the possibility of 'definitive self-exclusion from communion with God and the blessed'. We should note that the Catechism here does not say that any human being has actually gone to hell, only that it remains a possible human choice, and it sees in the Scriptures' teaching on the subject an urgent call to responsibility and conversion (1036).

Underpinning all that the Church teaches about death, resurrection and judgement, however, lies not fear but a great hope for a new heaven and a new earth: judgement is, in the end, an Easter theme and a creation theme. This expectation of the new Jerusalem, the restoration of all things in Christ, is, paradoxically, not 'otherworldly', but an affirmation of faith in the dignity, worth and ultimate destiny of this world which is passing away. Our hope for the new heaven and the new earth is an incentive to make of this earth a sign of the world to come, to make it more transparent to the love of God which will one day be all in all. And so, in the words of *Gaudium et Spes*, the Catechism sums up the Christian meaning of this hope:

> Far from diminishing our concern to develop this earth, the expectancy of a new earth should spur us on, for it is here that the body of a new human family grows, foreshadowing in some way the age which is to come. That is why, although we must be careful to distinguish earthly progress clearly from the increase of the kingdom of Christ, such progress is of vital concern to the Kingdom of God, insofar as it can contribute to the better ordering of human society. (1049)

AMEN

The Catechism began with an exploration of what it is to believe, and the word 'Amen' in Hebrew comes from the same root as the word to 'believe'. The Creed, like the Bible, ends with the word 'Amen', the word Jesus used when he wished to emphasize the trustworthiness of his teaching (1063). To believe is to say 'Amen', 'Yes' to God; but as we saw in our discussion of belief at the beginning of this book, underlying our every 'Amen' is God's Amen, his 'Yes' to us in Christ. The journey of faith, then, begins and ends with 'Amen' – God's overwhelming invitation to share his life in Jesus Christ, his 'Yes' to us, and our loving and grateful 'Amen' of acceptance. In uttering that 'Amen', we move beyond words, to life itself. The Christian's *life*, says the Catechism, is the real 'Amen' to the 'I believe' of our baptismal profession. As St Augustine says,

> May your Creed be for you as a mirror. Look at yourself in it, to see if you believe everything you say you believe. And rejoice in your faith every day. (1064)

Amen

NOTES

1 Yves Congar, *Called to Life* (New York, 1987), p. 60: Congar provided a useful review of Catholic thinking about the Spirit in the first volume of his three-volume work, *I Believe in the Holy Spirit* (London and New York, 1983).

2 Catherine Phillips (ed.), *Gerard Manley Hopkins* (Oxford, 1986), pp. 158–9.

3 Congar, *I Believe in the Holy Spirit*, vol. I, p. 164. The prayer was used by Pope Paul in his instruction on the place of Mary, *Marialis Cultus*.

4 I have made my own translation from the Italian text .

5 *I Believe in the Holy Spirit*, vol. III, p. 149.

6 Exodus 33:7–10; Numbers 9:15–23.

7 What follows is indebted to Congar's essay, 'The Spirit in action' in *Called to Life*, pp. 60–74.

8 Hans Urs von Balthasar, *Elucidations* (London, 1975), p. 70.

9 For all this, see his essay on 'The Marian principle' in *Elucidations*, pp. 64–72.

10 See Henri de Lubac, *The Church: Paradox and Mystery* (Shannon, 1969), pp. 30–67.

11 Classically in Henri de Lubac's masterpiece, *Catholicism* (English trans., London, 1950), chapter 7.

12 Augustine, *Retractions* 2, 18: see the excellent discussion of this issue by Bruce Harbert, 'Mother, City and Bride', *Priests and People* (August/September 1995), pp. 320–5. The Catechism discusses the holiness of the Church in more detail in paras 823–829.

13 Aidan Nichols, *The Theology of Joseph Ratzinger* (Edinburgh, 1988), p. 97.

Index